CHRISTIANITY AND THE BUSINESS WORLD

UNVEILING GOD IN THE MARKETPLACE

ADENRELE ADENIRAN

CHRISTIANITY AND THE BUSINESS WORLD
Unveiling God in the Marketplace

ACKNOWLEDGEMENT

Jonathan Haidt, quoting a former graduate student said, "We don't express gratitude in order to repay debts or balance ledgers, but rather to strengthen relationships."

There are a lot of people I would want to say a big thank you to for the publication of this book.

Chiefly, and most importantly, God, for giving the strength and wisdom to go through this project, despite numerous challenges and obstacles.

My lovely wife, Aderonke, for her input at various stages in my life since becoming a part of me.

My lovely daughters, Rolake and Derin, for warm words of encouragement which at times seemed innocuous, yet had a profound impact on me.

A very good friend and brother, Gbenga Akinrodoye, for his time in mulling over the concept of this book and rigorous discussions that significantly impacted the execution of this project.

Kenneth Nkemnacho, for his wise counsel and assistance. A big Uncle and esteemed brother, Professor Olukayode Oladipo, a man of intense intellectual capacity, who made himself available to advise and encourage.

I also appreciate some of my very good friends who stuck by me through a challenging time, and by their steadfastness proved a source of inspiration and encouragement - the indefatigable Olabode Oladipo (La Buddy), Jacob Ogogo, Ayodeji Opawole, Seye Ogunleye, Adetokunbo Ajayi, Abiodun Adeniran, the late Mobolaji Osinowo (Brother you are gone but not forgotten - RIP), Segun Olawepo and Ayodeji Bowale.

My profound gratitude to my parents, Isaiah Adeoti and Modupe Cecilia Adeniran. My parents-in-law, Dr and Mrs Robinson Adegoroye; Babatunde and Toyin Kitoye; Adeniyi and Seye Adegoroye; Yinka and Sayo Adegoroye; and Bukola Adegoroye.

How can I ever forget my siblings or thank them enough for their unflinching support; my solid rock of a big sister, Folake Adeleke; her husband, Adeniyi; Damilola and Dumininu Aderemi, for encouragement and engagement, which always proved intuitive. Thanks, Tubosun and Olumide, for always watching my back.

Also a dear aunt, Mrs Monisola Owolabi, and Professor Owolabi, for their immense support. Thanks also to good family friends (that cut across generations), Engineer and Mrs Yemi Esan.

This book would not be possible, without the help of Susan and David Ekundayo. You worked in making it readable. Thanks. Last but not the least, Adeola Oguntoyinbo, for her kind and gentle advice to getting to this milestone.

Contents

INTRODUCTION

For as long as I can remember I had always wanted to put my thoughts down in the form of a book (or books, because I want to do more than this); to express myself and record, for posterity, some of my thoughts.

And as long as I had considered it, I had always put it off until later, with the excuse that the time was not right. Well, that was beginning to look like procrastination. So, in 2013, I got my pen out and started scribbling down my ideas which culminated in this book. You may ask, 'Why spend five years writing just one book?'

Actually, I wrote a substantial part of it then. However, for some reason, the work was kept in the cooler. Sometime in 2017, I was reading a book, "The Righteous Mind: Why Good People Are Divided by Politics and Religion", by Jonathan Haidt (recommended by Feyi Fawehinmi). A name kept coming up, which I knew I had read about extensively somewhere else and made an impression on me—Émile Durkheim. That, coupled with other factors, made me dust-up my manuscript and begin the process of bringing the work to fruition.

I hope my modest contribution to knowledge enhances our understanding of where we situate God in the Marketplace and how God, as the Creator, always has the bigger picture, even when we cannot see or understand.

In Chapter One, we ask what is Religion? Is it still relevant today? Has the age of enlightenment consigned religion to the backstage of history? Does Man need religion to survive? How has it shaped the world we live in – for good or bad? Some of the answers try to situate some of these questions.

Chapter Two narrows down the broad perspective of religion to Christianity. What is the Church (or someone might say, Who)? Is the Church a building or a mass of people? How does it function? What are the intricacies that give her a supernatural aura? How is this Church connected to the One who is called the divine God, or are they not connected? The history and the place of the Church today is also discussed.

Chapter Three examines the concept of the Marketplace. How is it defined? To what good is the Marketplace? If we profess to be Christians, can we/should we operate in the Marketplace? How do we operate? And how can we operate in the Marketplace and still keep our commitment to God?

In Chapter Four, we take an in-depth look at the relationship between the Marketplace and the Church. Earlier, we mentioned that the Church is more than the physical structure. So, how does this body we call the Church relate with the Marketplace in such a way that there is a symbiotic relationship between them? What lesson does Jesus Christ, as the head of the Church, leave for us as Christians on how to interact and live within the confines of the world?

Chapter 5 concludes by looking at what role the Church is playing in establishing God's Kingdom here on earth. How do we do this without getting ourselves entangled with the world? What meaningful impact can the Church bring to the Marketplace? In being a light to the world and salt to the earth (light brings clarity, salt preserves), do we as Christians fulfil this function in our interaction with the world (Marketplace)?

Finally, I pray this book blesses you in reading as it has blessed me in writing it; that it equips you into becoming an efficient Christian worker, able to rightly divide the word of Truth to glorify our Lord Jesus Christ in the Marketplace.

CHAPTER ONE

WHAT IS RELIGION?

Religion is primarily concerned with the fundamentals of human existence. It attempts to address crucial questions and issues such as the creation of the world, the meaning of life, life after death, ethical living and personal happiness.

Religion has never been solely a cerebral affair; concerned only about abstract ideas. It has been and continues to be the lifeblood of societies all over the world, providing communities with meaningful rituals, colourful festivals, and pilgrimages to sacred places. Although religion has its dark side and can be used to bolster intolerance and unbridled nationalism, its power to inspire acts of charity and great works of art is unrivalled.

When Friedrich Nietzsche (1844–1900), the German Philosopher, pronounced "God is dead! God remains dead!" through the character of a madman in his book, "Joyful Wisdom", he seemed to sum up the prevailing spirit of his age. During the 19th century, the progress of science and rise of industrial societies in the West led many thinkers to believe that religion was indeed coming to an end. Science, with its ability to explain so many mysteries of existence would, they argued, convince people that they did not need to look to God for guidance.

DECLINE IN THE WEST

Apart from Nietzsche, other 19th century thinkers scrutinised the notion of God and the place of religion in society. Some, such as the German revolutionaries and thinkers, Karl Marx (1818–83) and Friedrich Engels (1820–95), developed the theory of religion, now called "Projectionist", which was first proposed by the philosopher Ludwig Feuerbach (1804–72). According to this theory, God was not an objective reality independent of human beings; on the contrary, God was a creation of the human mind, a figment of the imagination. People simply projected onto this "illusion" human qualities, such as compassion, that they regarded as ideal.

But what gave rise to this theory of an "illusory" God in the first place? For Marx and Engels, it was clear. They believed that the alienation ordinary working people suffered in capitalist societies made them turn to religion for comfort. Religion was the "Opium of the people", a drug that soothed their pains. Once capitalism has been destroyed they said, religion would be discarded.

However, their prediction appears to have at least been partially disproved by the rugged survival of religion in the former bastions of communism in Eastern Europe, and what was the Soviet Union. By contrast, the distinguished French Scholar and sociologist Émile Durkheim (1858–1917), did not believe that God could be so easily dispensed with.

Durkheim proposed that God was a product of society and that when a society worshipped God, it was actually worshipping a projection of itself. By this, he meant that when communities gather on important occasions they naturally give rise to collective sentiments and rituals which take on a sacred character and a life of their own, independent of those who created them. In this way, a rich store of symbols, rituals, and beliefs emerge which bond people together.

The general feeling that religion was in decline continued into the 20th century. Sigmund Freud (1856–1939), the founder of psychoanalysis, for example, was concerned about the effect of the demise of religion on society. In "The Future of an Illusion: Civilization and its Discontents and Other Works", Freud stressed that although religion could have its negative and destructive aspects, it helped to make civilisation possible. Without it, Freud argued, life in society would be impossible unless everyone was educated to behave morally.

THE PURPOSE OF RELIGION

With the changing demographics of religion in the world—the increase of Christianity in the developing world and the rise of Eastern religion in the West—it may be asked what purpose religion plays in peoples' lives. What question does it answer? What is its appeal? Religion's function has been debated since the 19th century by various scholars, and one of the most interesting and influential theories was developed by Émile Durkheim. He believed that religion had two main functions: cognitive and practical.

By cognitive, Durkheim proffered that religion makes the world intelligible to people, providing them the notion of time and space, cause and effects, and the ability to think about, as well as, understand the nature of society and the world. Religion is like philosophy and has a mental dimension that involves faith, ideas, dogmas, theology and reason.

That said, Durkheim, among others, felt that religion's ability to explain the everyday world had been largely taken over by science and secular philosophy. Religion's practical function—helping people conduct their lives—Durkheim believed, would continue to be of the utmost importance; a fact that he felt critics of religion often overlooked at great

11

cost to society. He said that through its rituals, religion releases energy within the committed followers of a religion in a particular community. This energy gives rise to a sense of security, happiness, belonging and inner strength.

In this way, religion functions as a sort of social cement; uniting people of the same society thus binding them together with a common set of ideas, norms of behaviour and duties. Durkheim was eager to emphasise this unifying element and spoke of religious beliefs and practices, "Uniting into one moral community called a church, all who adhere to them."

Many contemporary observers, however, think that religion has lost this unifying function. This is because modern society is so diverse and pluralistic that it is almost impossible for any religion to hold it together. Also, many aspects of society, such as the economy, education, politics and the Law, depend on technology and reason, rather than belief in God for their functioning.

Nevertheless, there are parts of the world where religion, combined with nationalism, fosters cohesion and unity, e.g. the Catholic Church in Poland, and Shiite Islam in Iran. On the other hand, in places such as Lebanon and Northern Ireland, both suffering from internal strife, religion appears to bind some communities together but divide them from others within the same country.

UNITY AND IDENTITY

There are societies, particularly in the non-Western world, such as Muslim Iran and much of Africa, where religion continues to serve as a "Sacred Canopy" overhanging the world. Both its explanatory and unifying roles remain vitally important; and in a rapidly changing world, religion in many places—especially Africa, Iran and Latin America—serves as a reassuring link with the past, often idealized as a glorious era: secure, meaningful, without evil and enjoying super-natural approval.

By contrast, in much of the Western world, religion no longer explains the mysteries of existence nor, in many places, does it continue to function as a form of social cement. Nevertheless, many still participate in some form of religion, although this increasingly takes place in the private sphere—involving, for example, an informal gathering for prayer and meditation, sometimes in private homes. Indeed, there seems to be a paradox at the heart of modern society: the greater the influence of science and technology, the more people turn to religion, even if it takes a non-traditional form.

Towards the end of the 20th century, however, it could be said that in many parts of the world, both God and religion were in excellent health. In the West, the status of religion is complex. In most of Europe, the number of adherents of the traditional Christian denominations such as the Catholic, Orthodox and Anglican Churches, had declined. In the United States however, the traditional church still retained sizeable followings. Catholicism continues to hold its own though and missionary movements are growing; especially those connected with Protestant churches as Pentecostalism thrives in some regions.

THE ROLE OF RELIGION IN EUROPE

To understand what Europe positively stands for, we need some information about religion, specifically, Christianity.

13

Five things that are often associated with Europe are Human Rights, Europeanness, Democracy, Distinction between Public and Private lives; and the Character of Modern European Art and Literary Culture.

Basic to all five aspects of identifying what is different about modern Europe and its post-colonial legacy across the Atlantic and elsewhere, is the belief that what is most uniquely human is a capacity for self-creation—for the making of choices that will establish a secure place in the world and shape an identity that is not determined from outside. This is determined by social power that acknowledges no accountability, or by doctrines and models that have no public evidence to support them.

If an individual decides to allow his/her identity to be determined hence, that is no doubt their business, but it is not something that anyone can rightly expect public authorities or the government to support or enforce or be a nanny state.

Public life organises the aspirations of individuals in such a way that they don't want interference with each other too dramatically, leaving what is supposed to be a reasonable amount of private space in which various individual preferences can be achieved.

It is in this sense that the essence of the human task is defining you. So, in Europe, you are allowed to define yourself in whichever way you want, insofar as it does not in any way impinge on another person. This is at the heart of the modern European enterprise and it is what sets it apart from both traditional societies and modern ideologically defined societies.

In traditional societies, a human being would be defined in relation to other human beings and their given roles and tasks. The whole complex of human associations is defined in

14

relation to a "sacred order" —the balance of things as defined by the will of God or the gods; the eternal harmony of all beings, the Tao of Chinese philosophy; or the logos of the ancient Stoics.

Within such a framework, fewer questions are asked and man is thought to be controlled rather than exercising control. This has its advantages as well as disadvantages. The disadvantage involves building a myth around what is not understood, rather than engaging and finding answers. And, insofar as the project of 'self-creation' challenges the priority of an external creating purpose outside this universe, it looks as though European modernity is basically hostile to any religious sense of the world and of human destiny. For many in the modern West, that is not, of course, a problem; it simply reflects the unstoppable advance of the demystifying of the world and the removal of authorities that work without rational accountability.

The obvious direction of human history is towards a world in which there is a level playing field; a universal space into which an individual may move and stake their territory. The government restrains excessive bids or claims that threaten others within this territory. But, this tidy summary conceals two major problems that we cannot indefinitely avoid discussing.

The first is simple: the fact that this model remains the preferred worldview of a prosperous minority of the human race (which can be described as the 1 percentiles); and shows little sign of being voluntarily adopted by others.

The sociologist, Grace Davie, has written about the 'European Exception' in relation to the patterns of religious commitment and practice in our world. She, of course, compares this to the statistically high level of religious practice in the United States. However, it may be suggested that since religion in the United States is characterised by many deeply untraditional features, by a sort of market principle of maximum variety and choice, it is itself as untypical as Europe in the context of what the rest of the human race thinks about religion. If religious commitment is, first and foremost, an individual's private choice, then, never mind whether the choice is yes or no, the principle is the same.

However, the second problem from which we are tempted to turn our eyes away from is the internal strain that is manifest in the way in which the 'European' model works in Europe and, more significantly, abroad. Some recent historians of Christian mission have located the missionary movements within the context of what they call the great European migration—the immense cluster of social and economic processes which, from the late Middle Ages onwards, took Europeans to other parts of the world, most often as conquerors or colonisers.

The emergent culture of Europe assumed that it had universal validity, but in practice this also meant that those who knew this culture as insiders, those who 'owned' it for themselves, had the right to decide how it should work; while those outside the European household had to be content with the structures imposed by insiders (occasionally with the promise held out that outsiders might one day become insiders). The effect was dramatic. The slave trade developed as a major international commercial concern at just the time philosophers were becoming increasingly eloquent about the universal human birth right.

The process began by which local economies were inexorably drawn into the mechanisms of transnational business—the material resources of the globe came to be seen as a virtually limitless warehouse for development. As is widely recognised, the European mind-set described has its beginnings in certain aspects of Christian language and belief, but also in the sheer social fact of how the Christian Church thought of itself in its earliest years.

Christianity was always a religion of conversion, and that means that it has always proposed to human beings that what has been taken for granted about their identities, their possibilities or their relationships is not necessarily fixed and final. Conversion is choosing to be different; it is stepping out of what you know and own, to a God who is better and superior to the indigenous gods. The early Christians had to navigate their way in bringing about the lifestyle and workings of their faith in such a way as not to subvert the entire fabric of social morality.

RELIGION AND SECULARITY IN THE WEST

The loss of religious influences over society (secularisation) in the West round about the 20th century started in the 18th century with the age of enlightenment. However, the trend in the early 1990s does not necessarily reflect a straight forward decline in belief or spirituality.

In Western Europe, many people, although nominally Christian, have, to all intents and purpose, left the old established Christian denominations. In Sweden and Denmark, for example, less than 5% of the population participates in church worship regularly and the situation is similar elsewhere. In France, once the foremost Catholic country in Europe, if the decline in church-going continues there would be more practising Muslims than Catholics.

There are, however, exceptions in Malta, the Republic of Ireland and to a lesser extent, Italy.

In the United States, 50% of the adult population still practises a religion of some type regularly, and certain Christian denominations, such as Catholicism, continue to grow.

Although many established churches in the West are in decline, they continue to gain ground in other parts of the World. And ironically, as Christianity directs its zeal more towards the developing world, religion such as Islam, Buddhism, and Hinduism, as well as movements derived from them, are making significant impact in the West.

THE FUTURE OF RELIGION

How religion will fare in the future, and, if it survives, what form it will take is difficult to predict. In the 1960s, some Christian theologians and social scientists predicted the end of Christianity by the year 2000; and there are other scholars such as Paul Van Buren (1924 – 1998), who claimed that the idea of a transcendent God, beyond the sphere of human existence, was meaningless to the modern secular person. They said that God had "withdrawn" altogether to allow people space and scope to exercise responsible choices for their lives.

Those theologians who espoused this view were trying to emphasise the necessity of a faith centred on Jesus Christ that was appropriate to a world that has "come of age". Even those who were in disagreement suggested that new ways of thinking about God were essential if people in the modern world were to retain a belief in God.

The Christian missionary movement is a global success story even though an estimated 70 countries are closed to all foreign missionaries. In the United States, there are almost 800 Protestant agencies, supporting some 70,000 overseas representatives. Since the 1980s, while the number of European missionaries has remained more or less the same, the number of American Protestant missionaries has risen by 80%. Much of this output emanates from California, which has the largest concentration of Protestant missionary organisations in the world. Modern Christian missionaries often come from prosperous churches and benefit from the latest technology; as did their 19th century counterparts, who used lantern slides and gramophones in the field.

The role of religion in the Christian traditional form has mostly diminished in the West. However, there is an exponential increase of the Christian faith in Africa and Latin America, whilst an increase of the Eastern Religion is seen in Europe. What this points to is the existence of an aspect of man that yearns for the divine; and this yearning is unquenchable with material things (money, wealth, cars, and fashion). There is a part that wants love, acceptance, peace and respect, which are by-products of religion; or a consciousness that we need to live for others, rather than for ourselves; and there is also a spiritual aspect to man.

CHAPTER TWO

WHAT IS THE CHURCH?

The Church is the Christian body, which has relevance now and in the life hereafter. The Church has come a long way from its inception to date and along the way. It has been battered, bruised, and persecuted, but it is still standing, and I believe will continue to stand, till she (the Church) becomes the bride and Christ, the bridegroom.

When we understand what or who the Church is, we can then begin to espouse and expand the horizon of what its function should be and how it can influence society.

The Church, for some, is the physical structure we see, the mosaic structure, cathedrals with long high beams bedecked with stained or patterned glass, some of which have been around for forever. This is correct, but only up to a point.

The Church can also be described as the body of Christ, where 'body' here refers to both the mass of people who come together in a communal way for fellowship and the anatomic body of Christ, in which he lived while on earth, died, was buried and then resurrected. The Church in the context of this book will refer to both, the mass of people, who in Antioch were later referred to as, Christ-like Christians; and the institution or organisation that makes up what we refer to as, The Church.

EMERGENCE OF CHRISTIANITY

About 2000 years ago in Judea, a provincial backwater of the mighty Roman Empire, an itinerant Jewish teacher and healer named Jesus of Nazareth preached a set of dynamic spiritual truths that became among the most influential words ever uttered. Jesus was considered by his disciples to be the Christ, the "Anointed One", or the Messiah, who would usher in the period of God's reign on earth. After Jesus' death, His followers, called Christians, proclaimed His miraculous resurrection. They steadily multiplied in number, and in the fourth century BC, the religion they professed was adopted by the Emperors of Rome.

For about 250 years under the Roman Empire, Christianity was a despised and persecuted sect. But when the religion was embraced by the Emperor Constantine in, or about 312 AD (he believed the Christian God helped him in winning a crucial battle), its future became inseparable from that of the Roman State that adopted it. There was benefit for both parties; Christians gained protection, respectability and eventually significant political power. The Church, in turn, gave the state legitimate political and spiritual influence.

Two thousand years after it was founded, Christianity (about 2.4 billion followers) now has more followership than any other religion and is established all over the world. As a result, it has had to adapt to a wide range of social conditions—persecution in China, active support in England, its closeness to the late tsar, Nicholas II and hostility by Lenin and Stalin, who like Karl Marx, believed religion was an opium of the poor. This has added both to its myth and attractiveness.

In 1054, the Church was rent asunder by a division that still has profound repercussion today. It marked the beginning, as distinct entities, of the Roman Catholic and Orthodox churches. This division did not happen out of the blue, but was the culmination of differences in the cultural, linguistic, spiritual and political traditions that had grown between the Western and Eastern halves of Christendom.

During the 16th century, Europe was rocked by a number of reforming movements that challenged the Catholic Church, which had become worldly and consequently lost much of its authority. These movements, collectively known as the Reformation, altered the face of Christianity. They initiated a new set of relationships between people and God, and religious authorities and people, which gave birth to a new church known as Protestant, because of their "Protest" against the Roman Catholic Church.

The most important reforming movement was begun by Martin Luther (1483–1546), a German Augustinian monk of humble origin, who rose to become a Professor of Biblical Theology at Wittenberg University. Luther was appalled at the laxity of the Roman Catholic Church, especially at the Church's sale of "indulgences", by means of which people could buy salvation and escape the punishment of purgatory. At the same time, he was racked with guilt at his own sense of sin and inability to earn God's forgiveness.

As a result of his study of Paul's epistle, on which he also lectured, Luther became convinced of the great theological truth, "Justification is by faith alone". Dismissing the Epistle of James, with its emphasis on good works, as "An epistle of straw", he insisted that God's forgiveness could only be received as a divine gift through faith in Jesus Christ.

To many poor people who could not afford to buy indulgences, Luther's claim offered deliverance from the ever-present threat of purgatory, and revolutionised their image of God—an angry, implacable judge became a loving Father. At the same time, however, it threatened the power and wealth of the clergy, friars and ecclesiastical lawyers;

they were not ready to let either go without a fight. As with all schisms, this did not end well; with the reformers subdividing into different factions, each with its unique set of doctrines and ordinances.

The style and doctrines of the Christian Church are mostly reflected in four features: Initiation, Worship, Ministry and "Good works".

Christian missionary endeavours went hand in glove with the expansion of European trade and colonisation, particularly after the opening of the New World. The rivalry between the ambitious seafaring powers of Spain and Portugal was so fierce that in 1493 Pope Alexander VI was forced to divide the world into Spanish and Portuguese spheres of influence. To Spain fell all of Latin America except Brazil.

The Spanish authorities, both civil and ecclesiastical, set about exploiting their new dominions, and in this process the Franciscans played a key role, led by the energetic Friar De Zumarraga (1468 – 1548), whose genius for organisation was such that he could claim a million converts between 1524 and 1531, and a further 4 or 5 million by the end of the decade. However, this feat was both achieved and sullied by the wholesale destruction of native culture.

By contrast, Portuguese activity in Africa and the East was less zestful. Although a diocese was founded at Cabinda in the Congo in 1521 and another under the Jesuit influence in Mozambique in 1641, the Portuguese made little impression in Africa at this stage.

In India, Gao on the West Coast was the main centre of activity from 1534 onward, and from there Francis Xavier (1506–1552), a close friend of Ignatius of Loyola (1491–1556) began to work along the East Coast, establishing a bishopric at St. Thomas, just south of modern Madras.

Disheartened by a lack of support and by the Portuguese King's greater interest in exploiting trade, Xavier travelled in 1549 to Japan, hoping to find more fruitful and less trampled political turmoil. He and his followers achieved considerable missionary success.

The spread of Christianity in Africa has been a relatively recent phenomenon compared with the Church's effort in the Americas and other parts of the world. By the middle of the 18th century, except for the ancient churches of Egypt and Ethiopia, there were only a few isolated trading settlements or military garrisons where Christianity could be found in sub-Saharan Africa.

African missions first began at the end of the 18th century at the Cape of Good Hope on the southern tip of Africa, where a relatively settled and sophisticated European colony had been established since the mid-17th century. Missionaries faced extreme hostility from the settlers, who resented their attention towards the Africans, whom the settlers regarded as competitors for land.

During the course of the next century, three things changed this situation and the advancement of the spread of Christianity in Africa took off. The first was a renewed confidence in their own effectiveness on the part of the churches of the West, which related to their mainly successful efforts in the struggle to end the slave trade. The second was the association of evangelism with the expansion of trade; a link that was especially attractive to the rapidly industrialising countries of Germany and Britain. The third was the scramble for African colonies that gripped the major European powers in the late 19th century. This subsequently led to the imposition of European administration on virtually the whole of Africa, making the missionary almost indistinguishable, in Africa's eyes, from the colonial official.

Apart from Egypt and the Mediterranean Coast, Christianity had by the fourth century penetrated Nubia and Ethiopia, where it died out in the 16th century, but it did not spread further south until the era of the Portuguese expansion from the late 15th century.

In the 16th and 17th centuries, Christianity penetrated most deeply into the Congo Kingdom. Its presence in Warri on the Nigerian coast and Monomotapa was more superficial. Otherwise, it took root within the Portuguese colonies of Angola and to a lesser extent, Mozambique. Angola retains the largest degree of continuity with a pre-19th century church.

A new Christian era started with the settlement of Black Christians from Nova Scotia in Freetown, Sierra Leone in 1787; and a missionary advance inland from the Dutch and then British colony into Cape Town, effectively beginning with the arrival of J.T. van der Kemp in 1799.

New missionary societies—the London Missionary Society (LMS), Church Mission Society (CMS), the Holy Ghost Fathers, the White Fathers—began work in many parts of the continent as the 19th century advanced; while new missionary strategies were developed by planners such as Henry Venn (1796–1873) and B.D Comboni (1831–1881).

Early missionaries varied greatly. They included explorers and publicists such as David Livingstone (1813–1873), translators such as Robert Moffat (1795–1883), political activists such as John Phillip (1775–1851), and African converts such as Samuel Ajayi Crowther (1809–1891).

Apart from the extreme South and the horn of Africa, the interior was hardly touched before the final quarter of the 19th century. The missions founded in 1875 at the Lake Malawi and 1877 by CMS Buganda marked a new beginning. The next thirty years coincided with the political "Scramble for Africa"; missions were established almost everywhere and a vast process of church growth got under way. The principal factors in conversion were the bush schools, the catechists, the vernacular texts of scripture, hymns and the like.

Certainly with the ending of the colonial era, mainly in the 1950s and 60s, the newly independent States treated the mission churches with polite indifference. As their social role in the community was taken over, often less successfully, by the State and they were challenged by the African independent churches, the major churches were forced increasingly on the defensive. Perhaps it will take another generation of genuine African leadership to find a style and a voice that will match the historic traditions of the faith of that African spirituality.

The increase in numbers of Christians in Africa, one of the fastest growing part of Christendom, has centred on "churches" that have sprung up around certain charismatic individuals, such as Simon Kimbangu in Belgian Congo, Williams Harris in Ivory Coast, and Ayo Babalola in Nigeria. These prophet-based movements are sometimes referred to as African Independent churches, since they owe no allegiance to, and have indeed been persecuted by, mainstream historic churches.

CATHOLICISM

Catholicism is a word derived from the Greek, meaning "universal or general". In Christian terminology, it has come to have various uses:

27

(1) Of the Universal Church as distinct from local Christian communities.

(2) In the sense of "Orthodox" as distinct from heretical or schismatic.

(3) In historical writing of the undivided Church before the schism of the East and West, traditionally dated in 1054.

In general, in present-day usage, it is employed of those Christians who claim to be in possession of a historical and continuous tradition of faith and practice, as opposed to Protestants, who tend to find their ultimate standard in the Bible as interpreted on the principles of the Reformation of the 16th century.

The Catholic Church, also known as the Roman Catholic Church, is the world's largest Christian church, with 1.29 billion members worldwide. It is among the oldest institutions in the world and has played a prominent role in the history of Western civilisation. The Catholic hierarchy is led by the Pope and includes cardinals, patriarchs, and diocesan bishops. The Church teaches that it is the one true church divinely founded by Jesus Christ; that its bishops are the successors of Christ's apostles; and that the Pope is the sole successor to St. Peter who has apostolic primacy. There are a variety of doctrinal and theological emphases within the Catholic Church—including the Eastern Catholic Churches, the personal ordinariates and religious communities such as the Jesuits, Franciscans and Dominicans.

The Catholic Church defines its mission as spreading the gospel of Jesus Christ, administering the sacraments and exercising charity. Catholic worship is greatly liturgical, focusing on the Mass or Divine Liturgy, during which the sacrament of the Eucharist is celebrated.

Catholic social teaching emphasises support for the sick, the poor and the afflicted through the corporal work of mercy. The Catholic Church is the largest non-government provider of education and medical services in the world. Catholic spiritual teaching emphasises spread of the Gospel message and growth in spiritual discipline through the spiritual works of mercy.

"The Church as a global corporation", can this fit into a narrative here? The New York Times columnist, Bill Keller, recently wrote a piece, "Catholicism Inc.", in which he sees the Catholic Church, at least analogously, but in many ways literally as a global corporation. He sees a church that needs to update and upgrade its marketing—tainted by scandal and corruptionand willing to make some changes.

The Roman Catholic Church according to Daniel P Horan could be described as a global corporation, with a hierarchical structure of leadership that, can be argued, needs to reform from within. According to Micheal Useem, Director of the Centre for Leadership and Change Management at the Wharton School, the Catholic Church can learn a lesson or two from the examples of how Warren Buffet cleaned up Solomon Brothers after a bond-trading scandal; and Ed Breen revived Tyco International after its chief executive went to prison for theft. It would well serve both those who believe in the gospel and those who do not. For those who believe, it is further proof of the church cleansing itself from within; and for unbelievers, it is a demonstration of taking to correction, which opens the window for them to have a look-in.

However, in as much as it could be argued that the church as an institution needs reform, the central message which it offers—the message of salvation and redemption—should not be lost in the process. One of the proposals by Keller is for a smaller and leaner Church, a suggestion also made by the former pope, Pope Benedict XVI. A way of looking at this is to borrow Micheal Useem's analogy of the Nokia vs Apple concept. Nokia's strategy is to sell everyone on the planet a $20 phone; Apple's is to market a much pricier product for a more elite, high-income market.

So does the Catholic Church change its standard to be more inclusive, or does it hold its dogmatic line and appeal to a smaller but loyal base; can she strike a balance? Definitely, the Nokia-Apple analogy falls short of adequately capturing the moral and ecclesiological concerns that are intrinsically at play in a discussion about the mission and visible dimensions of the Catholic Church.

A second question is: how ready is the Catholic Church in allowing latitude within it? Take, for example, McDonald's— it has a basic and consistent menu around the world, however, it allows its franchises in particular areas of the world to adapt individual local menus. Would the Church continue to insist on the use of Latin in its Masses; incense and all? Is it prepared to incorporate some joyful unconventional music? Or allow women to serve in liturgy? And lastly, the Church could do with a bit of a public relations exercise. Its stock response to criticism from without has been to drop into a defensive crouch, stonewall or go negative. This could come across as arrogant, which is not very Christ-like.

Changes are not the problem; Keller is correct to note that the Church has done so, and will continue to change. Pope Benedict XVI's decision to retire is just one example. What should or could be changed is the real question. How the leaders of the Church engage the rest of the Body of Christ and more broadly the world is certainly something that should and could change.

As "corporate" as "public relations" sound, the Church has largely been bad at effectively getting its point across in a world that is not used to lengthy Vatican documents and arcane procedures for communication. Perhaps, part of the "New Evangelisation" has less to do with gathering the "lost sheep" or other such metaphors and more to do with how to express one's faith in the most cogent and understandable way today.

ANGLICANISM

The word was coined in the 19th century from the much older word "Anglican", perhaps under the influence of the contemporary French term, Gallicanism. It probably denotes the system of doctrines and the practice of Christians who are in communion with the See of Canterbury, but has come to be used especially in a more restricted sense of that system in so far as it claims to possess a religious and theological outlook distinguishable from that of other Christian communions— Catholic, Orthodox or Protestant.

The original formulation of Anglican principles is to be sought in the reign of Elizabeth I rather than that of Henry VIII or Edward VI, for it was under her that a via media between the opposing factions of Rome and Geneva became a political necessity and Anglicanism as a doctrinal system took shape. Its Formularies, including the Book of Common Prayer, the Ordinal, the Thirty-Nine Articles and the two Books of Homilies came from Elizabeth's reign as the basis of Anglican self-understanding, preaching and doctrines.

The Anglican Communion is an international association of churches consisting of the Church of England and of national and regional Anglican churches in full communion with it, and specifically with its principal primate, the Archbishop of Canterbury. There is no single "Anglican Church" with universal juridical authority, as each national or regional church has full autonomy. The status of full communion means, ideally, that there is mutual agreement on essential doctrines and that full participation in the sacramental life of each church is available to all communicant Anglicans.

With a membership currently estimated at around 85 million members worldwide, the Anglican Communion is the third largest Christian communion in the world, after the Roman Catholic Church and the Eastern Orthodox Churches. Some of these churches are known as Anglican, such as the Anglican Church of Canada, due to their historical link to England (*Ecclesia Anglicana* means "English Church"). For example, the Church of Ireland, the Scottish and American Episcopal churches, and some other associated churches have separate names. Each church has its own doctrine and liturgy, based in most cases on that of the Church of England; and each church has its own legislative process and overall Episcopal polity, under the leadership of a local primate.

The Archbishop of Canterbury, religious head of the Church of England, has no formal authority outside that jurisdiction but is recognised as symbolic head of the worldwide communion. Among the other primates, he is considered as primus inter pares.

The Anglican Communion considers itself to be part of the One, Holy, Catholic and Apostolic Church and to be both Catholic and Reformed. For some adherents, it represents a non-papal Catholicism, for others a form of Protestantism though without a dominant guiding figure such as Luther,

Knox, Calvin, Zwingli or Wesley. And for another group, their self-identity represents some combination of the two.

METHODISM

The primacy given to science and human reason in the West during the period known as Enlightenment in the 18th century posed an intellectual challenge to the Church. Many Christians, especially the Deists whose belief in God was based on reason, denied the irrational aspect of religion such as mysticism, miracles and prophesy. They preferred a cool "reasonable" Christianity that appealed to the mind rather than to the heart.

This trend provoked a reaction in the form of evangelical revival movements, particularly Methodism, which sought to breathe a new life into the souls of the believers. The revival movement that came to have the most influence was Methodism established in Britain by the Anglican, John Wesley (1703−91). It was named for the "methodical" study and prayer practised by members of the Holy Club, founded by Wesley at Oxford University in 1729. With this club, Wesley's aim was to bring together like-minded Anglicans. They all emphasised the necessity of personal conversion, attended by a heightened emotion, and the hope of personal salvation. Among Wesley's fellow founders were his brother Charles, who became famous for his hymn writing, and the talented orator, George Whitefield (1714−70).

In 1738, Wesley himself underwent a profound emotional conversion experience, during which he felt a sense of God's forgiveness of his sins. Three years later, he and his colleagues began an extensive missionary campaign all over Britain and Ireland.

Methodism spread to the United States through the efforts of George Whitefield, whose visits began in 1739. By 1770, Methodism had become well established east of the Mississippi and, through the energies of the British preacher Francis Ashbury (1745−1816), it spread to the Mid-West. The revivalist message that Whitefield preached—namely, that personal salvation comes only through God's grace and faith in Jesus Christ—was echoed in the preaching of the New England minister Jonathan Edwards (1703−58). The American revivalist tradition was carried into the 19th and 20th centuries by, among others, Charles Finney (1792−1875), an upstate New York Presbyterian, Dwight L Moody (1837−99), and Billy Graham (1918−2018).

The evangelical revival, however, went beyond its emphasis on personal salvation to include social involvement. At the end of the 18th, and throughout the 19th centuries, there were many evangelicals on both sides of the Atlantic who worked to improve provisions, care for the mentally ill, reform prostitutes, and provide for the blind and deaf.

PENTECOSTALISM

Since World War II, one of the fastest growing part of the Church has been the Pentecostal movement. Her adherents believe they can have the same experience that the first Christians had on the day of Pentecost (Acts 2:1-4), when they received the gift of "Speaking in tongues" from the Holy Spirit. Since the 1960s, the movement has become part of mainstream churches, including Roman Catholicism, where it is known as Charismatic Renewal.

Speaking in tongues, or glossolalia, is usually understood to mean speaking a strange language—an "Ecstatic utterance"—unknown to the speaker, which can be grasped only by those who have the gift of interpretation. Sometimes, it is associated with healing or with the "giving of the word". Pentecostals, whose worship is marked by exuberance and joy, also claim other gifts of the spirit, including prophecy, healing, and exorcism. They could be either conservative or fundamental, depending on one's view.

Pentecostalism or Classical Pentecostalism is a renewal movement within Christianity that places special emphasis on a direct personal experience of God through the baptism with the Holy Spirit. The term, Pentecostal is derived from Pentecost, the Greek name for the Jewish Feast of Weeks. For Christians, this event commemorates the descent of the Holy Spirit upon the followers of Jesus Christ, as described in the second chapter of the Book of Acts. For this reason, some Pentecostals also use the term Apostolic or Full Gospel to describe their movement.

These early 20th century Pentecostals were radical adherents of the Holiness Movement and were energised by revivalism and expectation of the imminent Second Coming of Christ. Believing that they were living in the end times, these evangelicals expected God to spiritually renew the Christian Church thereby bringing to pass the restoration of spiritual gifts and the evangelisation of the world.

In 1900, Charles Parham, an American evangelist and faith healer, began teaching that "speaking in tongues" was the Bible evidence of Spirit baptism. The three-year-long Azusa Street Revival in Los Angeles, California, resulted in the spread of Pentecostalism throughout the United States and the rest of the world as visitors carried the Pentecostal experience back to their home churches or felt called to the mission field.

While virtually all Pentecostal denominations trace their origins to Azusa Street, the movement has experienced a variety of divisions and controversies. An early dispute centred on challenges to the doctrine of the Trinity. As a result, the Pentecostal Movement is divided between Trinitarian and non-Trinitarian branches.

There is no central authority governing Pentecostalism; however, many of the over 700 denominations and a large number of independent churches are affiliated with the Pentecostal World Fellowship.

There are over 279 million (there is controversy as to the numbers, as the definition of a Pentecostal seems fluid) Pentecostals worldwide, and the movement is growing in many parts of the world, especially the global south. Since the 1960s, Pentecostalism has increasingly gained acceptance from other Christian traditions; and non-Pentecostal Christians in Protestant, Catholic, and Orthodox churches, through the Charismatic Movement have embraced Pentecostal beliefs concerning Spirit baptism and spiritual gifts. Together, Pentecostal and Charismatic Christianity numbers over 500 million adherents.

In the United States, Christianity in many forms and guises is part of mainstream culture. One way this has evolved has been the rise of tele-evangelists, one of which is Pat Robinson of the Christian Broadcast Network (CBN); founded in 1977. In Latin America, the Roman Catholic Church has been dominant ever since the coming of the Spanish conquistadors in the 16th century, accompanied on their voyages of discovery and conquest by Roman Catholic missionaries.

It is from a Pentecostal/Charismatic perspective that we shall be exploring the relationship between the Church and the Marketplace; its overlaps, complements and controversies.

CHAPTER THREE

WHAT IS A BUSINESS (MARKETPLACE)?

A Business can be defined as an organisation or economic system where goods and services are exchanged for another, or for money. Every business requires some form of investment and customers to whom its output can be sold on a consistent basis in order to make a profit. It could be privately owned, not-for-profit, or state-owned.

Note the mention of services exchanged for another. This trade by batter business method was the earliest form known to man when he was a tiller of the ground and gatherer of wood. This practice still exists today, albeit on a much more reduced scale because of the existence of printed currency.

From the time that goods and services were traded in early civilisations, people have been thinking about business. The emergence of specialist produces and the use of exchange were methods by which individuals and societies, in modern terms, gain a "Business edge".

The ancient Egyptians, the Mayans, the Greeks, and the Romans all knew that wealth creation through the mechanism of commerce was fundamental to the acquisition of power and formed the base on which civilisation would prosper. Money gave rise to the concept of "Value added"—selling an item for more than it cost to produce.

God made man and gave him dominion over the fish in the sea, the birds in the sky, livestock and wild animals, and over all creatures that moved along the ground. However, because MAN lost his place of fellowship with God due to disobedience, he was sent out of the garden, to be a tiller of the ground. It was out of his sweat that he would now bring forth from the ground; hence his state of dominion was lost.

Since he had to till the ground, he needed implements and tools; thus, the idea of exchange (batter) sufficed and this way of doing business was born. With more experience, he got better at tilling the ground and maintaining control over his environment, although this was now done with sweat rather than his state of dominion with God.

Life's processes start with an idea; similarly, your business is conceptualised—first in your mind—before crystallising into something palpable. All businesses start from the same point—an idea; what happens to that idea determines business success.

The conceptualisation state is the incubation period. At this stage, ideas are created and discarded eventually making your dream a reality. You consider essentials such as company name, Logo, financial structure, clientele, what segment of the market you want to operate in, processes, and I dare say, an exit "strategy". The idea of an exit strategy is not to frighten you out of what you want to do; rather it is to make you far-sighted.

The conventional image of an entrepreneur is of a strong-minded, positive risk-taker with a sense of destiny, seizing the ever-present opportunities. In the early days of a new business, the most valuable skill a founder can have is entrepreneurship—the vision to identify opportunities, and the willingness to take risks. Ernst & Young, 2011, identified entrepreneurs as people who are non-conformist, driven, tenacious, passionate, and focused, with an opportunist mind-set. Other studies report entrepreneurs as mavericks, unafraid of failure, and driven by a passion for success. Disciplined management skills and corporate expertise are required to co-ordinate a growing enterprise.

40

Creating an organisational culture that embraces teamwork and encourages creativity helps firms address the perennial question: "Is money the motivator?" Higher pay might encourage an individual to take a new job, it might encourage people to move a little faster or work a little harder, but people soon forget about the money and start to focus on other things, such as job satisfaction, job prospects, and life-work balance, amongst others.

Through tradition, history, and structure, firms build a sense of identity—a unique personality defined by the characteristic rituals, beliefs, stories, meanings, values, norms, and language—that determines the way "Things are done around here".

Since God is the author of business, it behoves us to look up to Him for inspiration and guidance. One may ask how He is the creator of business. Well, when he created Adam, he told him to have dominion, hence putting Adam in charge of everything and appointing him as the "First Manager". As a businessperson, you invest in trade and hope to make a profit. The reward could be lots in financial terms, or adequate, but you derive a sense of purpose in what you are doing.

One purpose for business is that it should provide a means of creating wealth for a better and equitable society. Things to guard against in business are greed, insufficient scrutiny of corporate affairs, and insensitivity to opinion. The end goal of business, especially as it concerns Christians, should not be to make profit alone. Rather, it should be for the advancement of God's kingdom on earth, as well as making the world a better place. It should also outlast you. For example, George W. Meck, the son of the pharmaceutical company founder, always insisted that medicine was for the patient, not for profit. In 1987, in keeping with this core value, his successor decided to give away a drug called Mectizan, which cures river blindness, an affliction in the developing world.

God has created you with great and special abilities, so you do not have to be a businessperson in order to succeed elsewhere in life. For example, being a great mum—raising generational leaders such as the mother of Charles and John Wesley, Susannah Wesley (1669–1742); and Mama Hilda Adefarasin, who has godly children. Susannah Wesley did exploits for God and Mama Adefarasin is still doing exploits for God! Talking of raising God's generals, she is not just a mother, but also a woman activist, and a former President of the National Council of Women's Societies.

From little acorns, mighty oaks grow. The multinationals and big corporations we see today all started from somewhere, with someone conceiving a vision, projecting that vision and making the vision outlast him/her. Your business can start as a Micro, Small or Medium Enterprise, and grow to become a blue chip company, or from a conglomerate into a multinational corporation.

MICRO, SMALL AND MEDIUM ENTERPRISES

SMEs (Small and medium-sized enterprises), as they are commonly called, are made of enterprises with employees fewer than 250 persons, having an annual turnover not exceeding 50 million Euros and/or an annual balance sheet total not exceeding 43 million Euros. In other parts of the world (i.e. Nigeria), the CBN (Central Bank of Nigeria) defines them as independent companies with about 11– 30 employees and an annual turnover of between N5 million–N500 million.

Micro enterprises have less than N5 million and less than 18 employees. They provide very important and useful links to the society and economic base of the country. They are employers of labour, thereby raising the Gross Domestic Product (GDP) of the nation. Again, using Nigeria as a test case, this group at the micro level can include, electricians, welders, vulcanisers, artisans, and panel beaters. Some of these vocations might sound strange to a person in the West, but, for the various functions they serve, they are vital to the economic activity of the nation.

BLUE CHIP

The term blue chip was first used to describe high priced stocks in 1923, when Oliver Gingold, an employee at Dow Jones, observed certain stocks trading at $200 or more per share. They are nationally recognised, financially sound, and well-established companies.

According to the Financial Times, they are stocks of a major company with a record of strong earnings, reliable dividend payment, and steady price performance. They are normally the largest capitalised stocks in a particular market and among the most widely traded. Blue chip stocks are seen as a less volatile investment than owning shares in companies without blue chip status because blue chip has an institutional prominence in the economy. The stocks are highly liquid (the degree to which assets or security can be quickly sold or bought in the market without affecting the asset price), since they are frequently traded in the market by individual and institutional investors alike. They have little to no debt, large market capitalisation, stable debt-to-equity-ratio, and high return on equity (ROE), as well as return on assets (ROA). The solid balance sheet fundamentals coupled with high liquidity have earned all blue chip stock the investment grade bond rating. It would be observed that by their position and strength, blue chip companies are "lifters and carriers" of the nation's economy. Examples of some of these companies are Coca-Cola, IBM, General Electric, Apple, and Dangote to mention a few.

CONGLOMERATE

A conglomerate is a company that comprises multiple different corporations. It can also be defined as a corporation consisting of several companies in different businesses. The most common type of conglomerate is a parent company with one or more subsidiaries that are partially or wholly owned companies. Such a structure allows for diversification of business risk, but the lack of focus can make managing the diverse businesses more difficult.

Corporations form conglomerates for a variety of reasons:

- The desire to become involved in a business that is different from the company's main focus.

- A desire to diversify so that losses in one business may be offset by gains in another.

- An intention to transition the company towards a new area of business.

- Attractive revenues, either historically or projected, from prospective subsidiary.

GROWING YOUR BUSINESS

Our IDEA (Innovation, Desire, Effort, and Ability) about business comes from what we have seen others do. If we grew up in an environment where order and discipline were strong attributes, such attributes can configure our mind and influence our conception and execution of our ideas. If we grew up in an environment where entrepreneurship was actively promoted and encouraged, we would tend to lean in that direction.

From the conception of the business, we begin to see how it grows. Scaling is how an organisation grows by becoming more efficient and profitable as it generates more business. Simply put, the business is able to take on more orders or produce more products, without eating up the additional profits by adding additional resources.

According to Entrepreneur magazine, nearly half of all new business start-ups fail within three years. Beating the odds at start-up is tough. First and foremost, an idea, no matter how good, must be combined with entrepreneurial spirit, defined as the willingness to take risk. Without entrepreneurial spirit, a great idea may never be pursued.

Good business leaders and managers are defined by certain traits, such as an eye for detail, organisation, communication, emotional intelligence and ability to delegate. Canadian business guru, Professor Henry Mintzberg proposed that business can be broken down into three categories: managing by information, through people, and through action.

The very best leaders, as Steve Job said, "Put a dent in the universe." These leaders are not bound by convention; they are able to think outside the box, embracing one-of-a-kind ideas that disrupt the status quo in their favour. In today's hyper-competitive market, the leaders we celebrate do not only out-think, outsmart and out-compete their rivals, they disrupt entire industries. They change the game.

Rarely, though, do leaders achieve greatness alone. Leaders rely on managers. While leadership is about vision, management is about processes, planning, budgeting, structuring and staffing—tasks that help an organisation to keep doing what it does.

EMOTIONAL INTELLIGENCE

One of the most important traits a leader should have is emotional intelligence. In his bestselling book, Emotional Intelligence (1995), Daniel Goleman describes the five domains of emotional intelligence (EQ): Knowing your emotions; managing them; motivating yourself; recognising and understanding people's emotion; and managing relationships. Without EQ, a gifted leader may just be a car crash waiting to happen.

HOW BUSINESS WORKS

The process of managing and establishing a business from start and growing it is quite complex. There are intricacies along the way that need to be learnt and understood, in order to have a successful business venture. It requires a different set of skills, knowledge, and experience from a mainstream operation, because the objectives must be achieved within defined limitations. These constraints include scope, time, quality and budget.

A business team might include people from diverse units, disciplines and multiple locations. Success in business involves not only overseeing the people working towards the company's objectives, but includes managing the risk, schedule, relationships, individual and team input, a range of stakeholders with vested interest, and financial resources.

Having seen what a business venture entails, it is important to note that success in business is tied to many threads— financial planning, marketing, communicating skills, people management, leadership and human resources— and it is a combination of these threads that result in a successful business. One of these traits, which would be studied further in this book, is leadership.

CHAPTER FOUR

CHURCH AND BUSINESS RECONCILED

In examining the relationship between Business and the Church, we would need to determine what roles they play, where they are complementary and where they contrast.

The Church transforms lives; Business transforms income and gifts/abilities. The Church makes disciples by focusing on missions; Business manages resources. The Church meets the need for biblical growth; Business meets people's need for changing product. The Church serves as a place for fellowship and communal growth; Business serves as an opportunity for career growth and fulfilment of ambition. The Church serves as a place for public worship; Business serves as a Marketplace, where there is profit and loss.

BUSINESS/CHURCH CLICHÉS

As Christians, we tend to use some words as clichés. These words have their equivalents in the business world. Looking at these words critically, we see that what we are saying is the same thing being said in the Marketplace. What are the similarities in these terms? Are they applicable to the Body of Christ? If they are, are they being used effectively? What are some terms used in the business world and what can we say are the equivalent terms in the Church? Are these words mutually exclusive, or are they interchangeable? Are we only dealing with schematics when we use them?

For instance, the word faith in the Church, is the business world equivalent of risk. Faith, can also be seen as having tenacity. The anointing could pass for gift, talent or genius, whilst denominations could pass for branding/brands. Deliverance means to become aware of something after a period of time, being responsive to its drawback due to having better understanding.

Often times, there are mergers and acquisitions in the Marketplace. In the Church, these could be compared to Churches under an apostolic covering or ordinance. The way we greet a first timer in a church is similar to how Tesco, Sainsbury's or Waitrose would arrange their products for maximum customer attraction.

The Chief Executive Officer (CEO) of a business is the chief operating officer, having other executives along the ladder. He has an aerial or overarching view of what is happening within the organisation. He is also responsible to both the customer and the shareholders. In the Church, mostly within the Charismatic or Pentecostal settings, you would have the senior pastor, associate pastor(s), elders or leaders, and ministries with people supervising such ministries. The pastor is accountable both to God and the congregants.

This hierarchical form of organisation is a common thread both in Business and the Church. Along this path comes the need for succession planning. Who are the leaders being groomed for succession or do we just rely on the Holy Spirit? Don't forget that Joshua was an understudy to Moses, Elisha to Elijah, and Timothy to Paul. Would this plan have to be from the Leader's immediate family, as in a son or daughter?

Some of what we might say the Church has gleaned from the Marketplace are ideas such as target market. Is the Church patterned in a certain way for a particular section of society? Mission Statements are commonplace with businesses. The idea of one-liners with churches also buys into this concept.

THE CHURCH/BUSINESS, A NEW WAY OF THINKING

Archbishop Vincent Nichols, of the Catholic Social Teaching (CST), in his analysis of what business needs to do better, says the common good and dignity of the human person are the two elements that must be at the centre of any business. The others being solidarity, subsidiarity, reciprocity, fraternity, and sustainability. The archbishop was addressing the Church sponsored conference, "A Blueprint for Better Business". The conference drew together many major businesses including Vodafone, Unilever, McKinsey, Barclays, Tesco, Lloyds and BAE systems.

Ethically, many will have problems with some of these companies but if the Church is to have an impact on the wider world, then there has to be constructive engagement, even with those some of us may not be agreeable with. The common good and dignity of the human person are central themes, underlining why the Church has a role to play in guiding the world out of its present economic morass. The CST definition refers to, "The set of social conditions which allows people more easily to develop individually and communally."

The dignity of the human person was another concept that had many struggling. Nicola Smith, Head of Economic and Social Affairs, at the Trades Union Congress (TUC) and Lord Maurice Glasman have both advocated that business should do more toward the greater good of society.

In Germany, employers and government regularly sit down with trade unions and discuss economic priorities. As Lord Glasman pointed out, in Germany, the trade unions agreed to take a pay cut in the boom years, helping set the country up to be in the relatively prosperous position it is now, compared to the rest of Europe.

One element Archbishop Nichols could have added was a reference to that element of CST that underlines the importance of trade unions to justice in the workplace. Importantly, the impact of climate change was also seen as a priority by Unilever, Vodafone, and McKinsey. The ethos of companies like Unilever and McKinsey seemed very much toward building long-term enterprises where the common good is a major driving force.

Dominic Barton, Managing Director of McKinsey, emphasised the damage done by the short term attitude in business. The power of the shareholders looking for instant returns is often not for the common good. Instead, the business should build a long-term enterprise that is good for the people who work for it and the community it operates in. So, it would seem there is some hope moving forward for a progressive moral voice in the business world.

In a BBC Radio 4 debate recently, Christian social entrepreneur, Lord Andrew Mawson, made some comment about the 21st century Church: "The churches in this country are in crisis. They are not engaging with a whole generation because they got caught up in the technocratic/bureaucratic world from the 70s. They have got a real problem.... Faith communities need to drop some of their ways of thinking and move into the modern world". Part of the reason the Church has not done this is that we are still hung up with an old belief system that equates success as not being very Christianly or pious as the case may be.

It should not be by setting up a soup kitchen seasonally alone that the Church engages with society. Rather a more holistic approach even in the realm of business is required.

How about the Church being involved in profitable ventures which raise finances for it and provide employment for the good of the society?

As Dr David Landrum, Director of Advocacy at the UK Evangelical Alliance, says; "Our most hurting and broken communities in the UK need Kingdom oriented businesses. When we talk about justice, restoration, and renewal of these communities, on the most practical level, alongside sharing the good news of Jesus Christ, we are talking about jobs and employment. If we want to see transformed lives, we need to see business as mission and take a lead."

The truth is that business provides a great way of building the Kingdom. The key question is this: if it is business that shapes the world, then why can't the Church work in and through business to shape the world for good and for God? Shaping it for good brings wealth creation in communities, with greater justice and relief from poverty for the world's poor, with the dignity of useful labour.

Shaping it for God brings "life in its fullness"; a life reconnected with the One who made us and loves us, bringing hope and meaning and purpose. All of that is good news and is the motivation for Kingdom building businesses. So, can the Church make the change that Andrew Mawson calls for?

Well, it seems that the tide may be turning. The "Business as Mission" movement has seen many Christians heading for the business world, choosing to run a business as their way of changing the world into a more Kingdom-like shape.

Recently it has been noticed that a new trend has emerged; churches are running businesses as a way of impacting their local community—the set-up of a milkshake bar by a church to provide training and employment to some local youngsters, and a fun place to hang out with others who are customers.

Churches are running coffee shops, and leaders of yet another church have set up an estate agency on the high street. These are real, viable, sustainable and profitable businesses with a Kingdom impact, and transformation is happening.

The world has a major economic problem at the moment, which is affecting the lives of many of the people around us. Surely, part of the good news should be that the Church offers real help with this problem—I think she is grasping the vision.

THE IDEAL IN THE BUSINESS WORLD

"As Christians, we have to define the role our faith plays in our business transactions", this according to business mogul and Chaplain, Dr Christopher Kolade, Nigeria's former High Commissioner to the United Kingdom, at a business luncheon. Are we, businessperson first, then a Christian; or a businessperson and a Christian; or a Christian first, then a businessperson? Whichever of these scenarios we fall into determines the role our Christian faith plays in influencing our business transactions.

There is often a wide difference between the methods actually employed in doing business and what they should be. Good men who are in the thick of the battle of competition and rivalry with other firms in the same line of trade are the quickest to admit this fact. They would gladly see things managed so that every employee is satisfied with his/her wages and hours of work; and every competitor and customer gratified by the treatment he receives.

Business as a Fight: "The truth is", says a recent eminent writer on this subject, "Modern business is a fight. At bottom, it is a question of strength and courage." In this fight there are all sorts of men engaged. Men, who are honourable and upright and who fight fairly, taking no mean advantage, yet fighting strongly for place, power and wealth. Over against this company of men are those who are fair only when compelled to be fair and who contend with any means, good or bad, for the objects which they seek to attain. This latter class upsets trade, causes great commercial and banking houses to fail, and casts suspicion upon all corporations, by the sale of watered and fraudulent stocks. It is this idea of business as a struggle which causes working men to strike, sometimes rightly, against great abuses; and sometimes wrongly, over minor matters which might easily have been adjusted if they had been taken up in the right way.

Business as a Service: So long as the ideal of the business world is that business is a fight, little can be done to improve the present conditions under which capital and labour work and suffer. War is costly and so far-reaching in its disastrous effects that it leaves a trail of misery behind it. Industrial war is no different. So, why look upon business as a fight?

Already a new ideal is before the world, that of service. This is what business really is. It carries things from the place where they are abundant to where they are not. It seeks to feed, clothe, house all mankind, and facilitate travel and commerce. Upon the earth, and in it, enough of all things have been provided for all its inhabitants—the table spread by God has been bountifully furnished—if only there were a proper distribution, no one need lack.

It is this matter of unwillingness to unselfishly serve others which slows down commerce today. When, however, men cast aside all other ideals save that of being of the largest service to their fellow men, we shall have a new order of things. Men will no longer seek to accumulate for themselves alone and the labourer will work with his full strength and a glad enthusiasm. No man ever did his best work without some great ideal before him which refreshed and quickened all his energies. If the business man would save himself from becoming sordid; and the poorest paid working man refrains from becoming sullen and hardened, they should keep ever before them this vision of service.

OWNERSHIP

If the ideal of service is accepted in the business world as true, then the question arises, what or whom should man serve? Should it be a thing—silver, gold, house or land? Should a man serve another man as a man? Whatsoever a man serves he becomes subject to; he is dominated by it and his thoughts go no further.

Every man is tempted to serve the lower instead of the higher. Jesus was tempted (Matt 4:1–11) with certain seemingly great and temporal advantages to relinquish His service to His Father, but He made it clear once and for all that the supreme object of service should be God (Matt 4:10), "Him only shalt thou serve." Paul also exhorts all men, in all occupations, to keep in mind first of all the service of God and of Christ, and to do whatever they do to God. Then, if they administer great or small affairs, if they are masters or servants, they will seek to please God and, having this higher ideal, will do far better work than they otherwise would in every sphere of life (Eph 6:7).

God, the Owner of All: God as sovereign, and over and in all, is the proper object of service for the businessperson. Nations have parcelled out the earth amongst themselves and claimed ownership. Men hold the titles of lands under the laws of the nations. Men dig, plant and reap, and call the products of the soil their own. But behind the titles of men and the claims of nations, God is the great proprietor.

The bible, speaking in various passages, talks about the earth being the Lord's, the cattle upon a thousand hills being His, as well as the silver and gold being his too (Psa 50:10).

Man is a tenant at the will of God: No man really owns the goods in which he deals or the lands to which he holds the deeds. He may be called away from temporary ownership at any time. It was asked, when a certain very rich man died, "How much did he leave?" The reply was, "He left it all, and he took nothing with him." "For we brought nothing into this world, and it is certain we can carry nothing out" (1 Tim 6:7).

Christ emphasised the uncertain tenure upon which all property is held by the parable of a certain rich man who had much goods laid up. He congratulated himself upon this fact and proposed to pull down his barns and build greater, saying to his soul, "Take thine ease, eat, drink and be merry," but God said, "Thou fool, this night thy soul shall be required of thee: then whose shall those things be which thou hast provided?" (Luke 12:16 –21).

TRUSTEESHIP

Man as a Trustee: There is no truth more clearly noted and stated in many ways in the Bible than the position of man as a trustee. Jesus used the parable of the talents to illustrate this great truth (Matt 25:14 −30). It is plainly taught in this parable that man is under obligation to God. No man ever brought himself into the world. No man ever originated his own talent; some men have been endowed with what seems to be greater possibilities than others.

To one man has been given the talent for administration, to another that of a ministering spirit, to another mechanical genius, to another that of wealth and to another the power of song or speech. But whatever the talent given, great or small, it is distinctly set forth in the New Testament that it is given in trust and is to be used in the service of Him who has bestowed it.

The businessperson is expected, by his Lord, to buy and sell, not for himself alone, but as a trustee. In this office, it is of great importance that a person is found faithful of the confidence reposed in him. A person in a trusteeship, if he is honest, will not waste or squander the property entrusted to his care. He will treat fairly and honestly all who work for him. Those working for him will feel that they are also trustees seeking to utilise their skills and time, so that the best interests of God and man may be served.

Man's right to hold property and do business is recognised by Christ. In the parable of the minas (Luke 19:12 −26), He commends those who used the money in trading to gain more; they rendered a good account when the nobleman returned. He condemns the man who having received one minas made no effort to increase it. He says, "If ye have not been faithful in the unrighteous mammon, who will commit to your trust the true riches" (Luke 16:11).

He made no demand of His disciples, as far as the record shows, to give up their property. The case of the young man of great wealth (Mark 10:17–27), who wanted to follow Christ, and of whom Jesus required that he should divest himself of his property, is fully in accord with Jesus' teaching concerning wealth and the holding of property. The key to the whole matter, on this point, is found in what Jesus says of this very case, "How hard it is for them that trust in riches to enter into the Kingdom of God" (Mark 10:24).

This young man did not possess his wealth but his wealth possessed him. He was the servant of his money. Jesus' teaching is that a man should hold money in trust. He warned men of the risk of possessing property, lest it become their master. Money, considered simply as money, is a hardening influence and in the restive desire to get more, the best things in men are quite sure to be eliminated. The danger lies in the power of money to gather affection and to absorb trust, thus displacing God.

The Reckoning: There comes a time when every trustee is called upon to render an account of how he has administered the business entrusted to his care. This time may be long delayed, and in the meantime many abuses may crop up, and it appears no account will ever be demanded. These conditions are plainly pointed out by Jesus in the parables of the vineyard (Luke 20:9 –16) and the tares (Matt 13:24–30), but it is also made equally clear that in the end, every man's work shall be judged.

In this reckoning, there can be no creative account of making things appear as they are not. There can be no juggling with the accounts. Every businessperson must show his books (Revelation 20:12) and how he has dealt with that which was entrusted to his care. In looking forward to the time of reckoning, men who are in offices of earthly trust pay careful attention to the investment of funds and painstakingly investigate the security offered. Jesus would have every man equally be careful in the investment of his time, labour, talent, and money as he will surely be called upon to give an account of his stewardship.

The time of reckoning is uncertain, but every business-person is expected to be ready for an investigation any time the examiner appears. The profit of business done as a service in the sight of God, is declared to be sure and large. Sacrifices made will be more than amply repaid (Matt 19:27 –29).

BUSINESS AND ITS CHALLENGES

It is a well-known fact that, in the business world at large, there is a very great percentage of failures and too many tombstones mark, not only wrecks of businesses, but also of character. The reason often given is that the eye is fixed too frequently and earnestly on immediate and large profits for self. But no man, who has openly and honestly sought to be of service to God and his fellow men in business, has ever been a failure. The real failure in business is a failure of character.

A businessperson may be humbled by unexpected circumstances or the fall of other firms but, if he keeps his character intact, he is no failure. On the other hand, a man who has taken selfish advantage of others may be made rich in goods, but he is a rank failure in character. The standard of character in business is, after all, the yardstick by which the small or the large dealer is judged; even by businessmen themselves. Business transactions are constantly being raised to a higher level by the enforcement of this standard.

The spirit of discontent and contention finds lodgement in the heart of the humblest working man, up through all grades, to that of the richest employer; for no man, however wealthy, ever thinks he has enough of this world's goods. Those who have the most are often the most eager in grasping for more. Courts of Law can only regulate the more flagrant outbursts of the prevailing sentiment, they do not and cannot remedy the causes.

Taking a cue from what Jesus teaches about loving our neighbour, Matt 7:12 states, "Here is a simple, rule-of-thumb guide for behaviour: Ask yourself what you want people to do for you, then grab the initiative and do it for them" (The Message translation). In order to rightly observe this rule, there must be first an avowed allegiance to God. "Thou shalt love the Lord thy God" (Matt 22:37) precedes the command to "Love thy neighbour." It is only when men love God aright and obey His commandments that they can come into proper relations with their neighbours.

Hence, in seeking God first and obeying the Golden Rule, the whole outlook of employer and employee will be changed. The attention will not be fixed upon the inequalities of life or the making of a fortune, but upon the desire to be of service. Each man will look into his work to improve it and seek to help his neighbour. Whatever the compensation, he will seek to do his best, serving as in the sight of God.

"A just consideration of the rights of others is the very beginning and end of true social economy." It is difficult to enforce any law which works against a public sentiment, but let the latter be in favour of the former and the law will enforce itself. Let the sentiment in the industrial business world be in favour of a supreme service and the difficulties and trials of strikes and lockouts would disappear. The energy, time and money spent in fighting could be turned to the benefit of employer, employee and consumer.

CO-OPERATION

Jesus never set class over or against class. He mingled with the wise and the unwise, the rich and the poor. He sought to draw men together in a common brotherhood. This brotherhood was not composed of employers or of men who worked at a certain trade, but of those who sought to build up the kingdom of righteousness. The world awaits the cooperation of all persons in the business world on the basis of love for each other and seeking the best interests of all concerned. This again is a sentiment, but it is one which must work against the prevailing sentiment of selfishness and greed if ever a better state of things is to be accomplished.

JESUS CHRIST, THE GREAT EXAMPLE AND LEADER

No man was ever so marvellously endowed with power as Jesus, yet that power was used for the good of mankind.

The man who follows Christ is the one who makes his business minister to the needs of men; helping to improve their conditions, whether they be rulers or the ruled. The glory is that, today, there are many men in the ranks of employers and employees who are trying conscientiously to carry out the Golden Rule—co-operating with their fellow men and following Christ in His business of ministering to them.

Examining the financial crisis from a religious point of view, a few questions arise. What for? What is growth for?

For what and for whom is wealth important? If it is essential to invest in certain kinds of productive ventures, how does this relate to the broader and long-term imperative of securing the funding of social care using sustainable shared resources, and accumulated wealth?

In the Christian belief, the world exists because of a free act of generous love by the Creator. God has made a world in which, by working with the limitations of a material order declared by God to be "very good", humans may reflect the liberty and generosity of God. Our salvation is the restoration of a broken relationship with this whole created order— accomplished through the death and resurrection of Jesus Christ and empowerment of His spirit—which should give rise to a community of mutual service and attention, the basic elements through which the human world becomes transparent to its maker.

INFLUENCE OF EARLY CHRISTIANS IN BUSINESS: QUAKERS AS A CASE STUDY

In England in the late 1640s, following the English Civil War, many dissenting Christian groups emerged, including seekers and others. A young man named George Fox was dissatisfied by the teaching of the Church of England and non-conformists. He had a revelation that "There is one, even, Christ Jesus, who can speak to thy condition" and became convinced that it was possible to have a direct experience of Christ without the aid of an ordained clergy.

The Quakers: In 1650, George Fox was brought before magistrates on a charge of religious blasphemy; it was here the magistrate first called him "Quaker" because I bade them tremble at the word of the Lord. Thus the name Quakers began as a way of ridiculing Fox, but was later accepted and widely used by the Quakers. Quakerism gained a considerable following in England and Wales and its numbers grew in leaps and bounds.

However, the dominant discourse of Protestantism viewed the Quakers as a blasphemous challenge to social and political order. It was not until, 1689, with the Act of Toleration, that the persecution stopped. One modern view of Quakerism at this time was that the relationship with Christ was encouraged through spiritualisation of human relations and the redefinition of Quakers as a holy tribe, "The family and household of God".

Together with Margaret Fell (1614–1702), the wife of a pre-eminent English judge, Fox developed new a conception of family and community that emphasised "Holy conversation, speech and behaviour."

In 1691, George Fox died. Thus, the Quakers movement went into the 18th century without one of their most influential early leaders. Thanks to the Toleration Act of 1689, people in Great Britain were no longer criminals simply by belonging to the Society of Friends (also known as Quakers). During this time, other people began to recognise Quakers for their integrity in social and economic matters. Many Quakers went into manufacturing or commerce because they were not allowed to earn academic degrees at that time. These Quaker businessmen were successful in part because people trusted them. Customers knew that Quakers felt a strong conviction to set a fair price for goods and not to haggle over prices. They also knew that Quakers were committed to quality work and that what they produced would be worth the price.

Quaker influence on Society: Some useful and popular products made by Quaker businesses at that time included iron and steel by Abraham Darby II and Abraham Darby III, and pharmaceuticals by Williams Allen. The Quakers succeeded in manufacturing and commerce and migrated to new territories, but they also became increasingly concerned about social issues, thus becoming more active in society at large.

During the 19th century, Friends continued to have an impact on the world around them. Many industrial concerns started by Friends are detailed in Milligan's "Biographical Dictionary of British Quakers in Commerce and Industry 1775–1990". They also continued their work in the area of social justice and equality. They made other contributions as well in the field of science, literature, art, law and politics.

In the realm of industry, Edward Pease (1767–1858) opened the Stockton and Darlington Railway in northern England in 1825. It was the first modern railway in the world and carried coal from the mines to the seaport. Henry Rowntree (1837–83) and Joseph Rowntree (1836–1925) owned a chocolate factory in York, England. When Henry died, Joseph took it over. He provided workers with more benefits than most employers of his day; he also funded low-cost housing for the poor. John Cadbury (1801–89), founded another chocolate factory, which his sons George and Richard eventually took over. A third chocolate factory was founded by Joseph Storrs Fry (1767–1835) in Bristol.

As previously mentioned, Quakers actively promoted equal rights during the 19th century. As early as 1811, Elias

Hicks (1748–1830) published a pamphlet showing that slaves were "prize goods", that is, products of piracy—hence profiting from them violated Quakers principles. It was a short step from that position to reject the use of all products made from slave labour.

Quaker women such as Lucretia Mott (1793–1880) and Susan B. Anthony (1820–1906) joined the movement to abolish slavery, moving them to cooperate politically with non-Quakers in working against the institution. Somehow, as a result of their initial exclusion from the abolitionist activities, they changed their focus to the right of women to vote and influence society.

Prison reform was another concern of the Quakers at that time. Elizabeth Fry (1800–45) and her brother, Joseph John Gurney (1788–1847) campaigned for more humane treatment of prisoners and for the abolition of the death penalty. They had moderate success in that Parliament did eventually pass legislation to improve prison conditions and to decrease the number of capital crimes.

In the early days of the Society of Friends, Quakers were not allowed to get an advanced education. Eventually, some did get opportunities to attend university and beyond, which meant that more and more Quakers could enter various fields of science. Thomas Young (1773–1829), an English Quaker, experimented with optics, contributing much to the wave theory of light. He also discovered how the lens in the eye works, described astigmatism and formulated a hypothesis about the perception of colour.

Maria Mitchell (1818–89) was an astronomer who discovered a comet; she was active in the abolition movement and the women's suffrage. Joseph Lister (1827–1912) promoted the use of sterile techniques, based on Pasteur's work on germs. Thomas Hodgkin (1798–1866) was a pathologist who made major breakthrough in the field of anatomy. He was the first doctor to describe a type of lymphoma named after him. John Dalton (1766–1844) formulated the atomic theory of matter, among other scientific achievements.

Quakers were not apt to participate publicly in the arts. For many Quakers, these things violated their commitment to simplicity and were thought too "worldly". Some Quakers, however, are noted today for their creative work, John Greenleaf Whittier (1807–92), an editor and a poet in the United States. Among his works were some poems involving Quakers' history and hymns expressing Quakers theology. Edward Hicks (1780–1849) painted religious and historical paintings in the naïve style; and Francis Frith (1822–98) was a British photographer whose catalogue ran into many thousands of topographical views.

At first, Quakers were barred by law and their own convictions from being involved in the arena of law and politics. As time went on, a few Quakers in England and the United States entered that arena. Joseph Pease was the son of Edward Pease. He continued in and expanded his father's railway and colliery business. In 1832, he became the first Quaker elected to Parliament. Noah Haynes Swayne (1804–84) was the only Quaker to serve in the United States Supreme Court, he was an Associate Justice from 1862–81. He strongly opposed slavery, moving out of the slave-holding State of Ohio in his young adult years.

CHAPTER FIVE

LEADERSHIP IN BUSINESS AND THE CHURCH

Jesus never died for any business; He died for the businessperson. For the past twenty years or so, the thinking of leaders and leadership has been pretty much one way—from business to the church.

Businesses deal with the same issues in people as the Church does: motivation, communication, organisation, vision, financial management, change, ethical decisions, how to control selfishness and self-interest (the flesh), and many other concerns. Businesses and the Church have a great deal in common. So should a church be run like a business?

Businesspersons at times see the Church as slow, unfocused, unchangeable, blind to opportunity, and sloppy in financial management. However, when we look at the flip side of business, using Lehman Brothers, Bear Stearns, and Enron as examples (these were large corporate organisations that collapsed due to financial infractions), we might be inclined to ask "What is so great about businesses that the Church should want to be like them? This is especially true when we look at the CEO model of a modern day business enterprise. This model is certainly more efficient than a shepherd-pastor model, but it is not found in scriptures. So, the question is, "Why can't we run a business like the Church? Why not look at what the Bible has to say about leaders and leadership and bring its truths to bear on business?

The Bible has a great deal to say about how to lead people effectively: the role of concern for followers (love), the place of truth in leadership (integrity), bringing order out of chaos (1 Timothy, Titus), leaders as models (1Timothy, Titus, 1Cor 11:1), leadership character (1Timothy, Titus), generational and gender relationships (1 Timothy, Titus), and many more factors, all of which would benefit business greatly.

TITUS AS A CASE STUDY

Using the book of Titus as our case study, what can a businessperson learn about leading from Paul's leadership memo to his trouble shooter, Titus? What can a business leader learn from a study of elders in Titus?

Now we must acknowledge that the question "Why can't we run a business like the Church?" is a rhetorical question, a take-off on the often asked question "Why can't we run the Church like a business?" Asking either of these question is like asking why not run submarines like an airplane. After all, both serve as means of transportation. We use both in fighting wars. Both have engines and propellers. Both have a captain and a crew. Both use radios to communicate. Both are dependent on radar. So let's run a submarine the way we run an airplane—it will end up at the bottom of the sea. Why? Because the differences between a submarine and an airplane are far greater than the similarities. Air and water are related, but very different elements, and to try to run both the same way despite some commonalities would be disastrous.

The differences between the Church and business are just as great as that between a submarine and an airplane. You can't run a church like a business because you can't manage sheep like you can an inanimate project. You cannot measure their effectiveness the same way. Some of the inefficiencies of the Church are built into the very core of its purpose—to transform people. Well, people can be messy, and you cannot dismiss a sheep like you can an unruly employee, not even the messiest of the lot. Churches and businesses have a great deal in common, but just like submarines and airplanes, their differences far outweigh their similarities. Yet, business can learn from the Church and vice versa.

In his short leadership memo to his young trouble shooter, Titus, Paul tells us what leaders do: Leaders do orderly things through exemplary lives. Paul tells Titus that he is to "Set in order what remains" (Titus 1:5).

From this we see the things leaders do:

1. Leaders do orderly things by transforming chaos into order. Some of the issues Paul wanted Titus to set in order included: focusing the church on truth, building healthy relationships among generations and gender, living in ways that express true character, doing good work, and unifying the church.

2. From this, it is clear that there was severe lack in the church. Issues such as false teaching, unhealthy leadership, ungodly living, selfishness, and disunity abound. Such matters guarantee chaos, and Titus' job was to set the churches in order. Are there any similarities between the causes of chaos or disorder in the Church and business? What kind of leadership do you think it takes to bring order out of disorder in the business setting? Paul reminds Titus that order will be restored by appointing elders (Team leaders). Without leadership, chaos prevails.

Leaders and Leadership transform chaos to order: Without leaders and leadership, chaos is certain. Yet, there are many who wrestle with the issue of leadership, because in their minds it means dominance and control. They feel weak, inferior, unable to entrust themselves to others, because they fear they cannot protect themselves and be safe. Perhaps many of these people have been the victims of leadership power play, and leadership that lords its authority over them rather than lifting them up to new levels of life and freedom.

Such people need to see leaders and leadership in a new light; in the light of Jesus' teaching leaders are servants—slaves ready to sacrifice themselves for their followers even as He did. Those are the kind of leaders Paul calls for Titus to appoint as we shall see when we consider the concept of leadership.

Still, others are rebellious and do not want to submit to anyone else or be held accountable. They are independent, self-willed (even when they cover it with God-words), and are too weak to be led. To say they are weak may surprise you since we tend to think of this kind of person as strong. But such people often do not have the strength of character to subject themselves voluntarily to leaders, especially if their leaders are their peers and more especially if their leaders are younger than they are. Such people are totally out of step with the New Testament, because the only kind of person recognised as righteous in the New Testament is the person who voluntarily subjects himself to all others in the body through the power of the Holy Spirit (Eph 5:22).

There are others who seek leadership, not because they want to serve, but because they are competitive, controlling and looking for a way to establish their own dominance, while hiding behind some kind of spiritual cloak. As soon as they get into leadership, they begin to bully the sheep and overpower them rather than care for and mature them in the path of righteousness and service.

None of these leaders is qualified to lead in the Church—or in business. Each of these leaders will mean failure for the Church or business that appoints them into these positions of authority. Such leaders—if we can call them leaders—will never bring God's kind of order that naturally occurs when human beings come together in a group out of the chaos. Without qualified and healthy leaders, disorder will persist.

By putting the appointment of elders first in his leadership memo, Paul establishes the reality that leadership is the primary issue when it comes to establishing the kind of order the Church (or business) needs in order to flourish. Order never comes of itself. Left alone everything atrophies in accordance with the law of entropy. Everything disintegrates into disorder unless there is a greater force at work to bring and hold the parts together. Unless the right hands take over—the right kind of hands—chaos will always overwhelm order.

CORE ELEMENTS IN LEADERSHIP

There are at least five things Paul says the right hand must do if order is to come out of disorder: Creation, Direction, Instruction, Protection and Formation. The primary responsibility of leaders in bringing order out of disorder may be summarised in saying, "Leaders fix broken windows". In other words, leaders create a healthy environment in which disorder is rejected and recognised as destructive to the well-being of the people and the institution they lead; broken windows are not acceptable.

Three things mark this healthy environment: Responsibility, Accountability, and Integrity. Leaders bring about order by creating an environment in which followers:

- Choose not to break windows but to clean up messes. So, they assume *responsibility* to pursue healthy living practices.
- Hold each other mutually *accountable* for their actions as they encourage each other to learn and to grow.
- Grow together in a heart for *integrity* in actions and relationship.

Some of the reasons we cannot run a business like a church include the fact that it would not be profitable. Church attendance is weekly, while a business operates 5 to 7 days a week; there is more passion and commitment in running a business; business is fear-driven as managers keep everybody afraid of losing their jobs, so employees are productive.

Business focuses on the needs of customers. Does this imply that churches don't? Probably. Many businessmen would say pastors have no idea what they face on a daily basis, and they are probably right. When both business and the Church are successful, they are a reflection of what is right. To be successful, both have to focus on why, what, and how they serve. This will show up in numbers for both, and success for both is often the reflection of one man. He must be a man among men who builds a team and releases others to play a vital role in light of their gifts and calling.

Most business leaders are driven by the fear that they will lose their position by appointing someone better than they are in leadership positions on their team. So they make fear-driven decisions to go with their power-driven and greed-driven decisions. While most ministry leaders don't make greed-driven decisions, they can be guilty of the other two.

Business and the Church have different purposes: making money vs making disciples. Is business all about making money? Are there no higher purposes for business? And are churches really about making disciples? What does that look like in the Church? Is this not a major problem? The Church is about keeping everybody happy rather than calling everybody to discipleship.

As Christians we can use business to make disciples. Business can be the bridge from the world to the Church; businesspersons are ministers to the world on behalf of the Church and the Gospel. The two are not in conflict or opposites; they work together—they are inter-woven. Businesspersons go out from the Church into the world and bring those from the world into the Church. The aim of the Church is to equip businesspersons to minister in the world, and the Church needs to learn how to do this.

The Church lacks the same kind of control that businesses have over people because it doesn't determine their financial well-being. The Church is a voluntary organisation, and you cannot fire volunteers. Or can you?

The products of the Church and business are different: eternity vs wood, hay, and stubble. Is that statement true?

Some business principles the Church can adopt include: Appointing leaders who bring order out of disorder (creative disruption), focusing on its purpose, keeping its promise, establishing integrity as one of its highest values, encouraging healthy relationship, and bringing unity to the company.

THE LEADERSHIP JUMP (CASE STUDY)

In his write-up on the Emerging Church, Jimmy Long, relates the dilemma of leadership today with an example of two of his friends: "I laugh so I wouldn't cry! Within twenty-four hours I had met with two of my best friends, Jonathan and Ken, who both happen to be pastors, in a church I know well. First, I met with Jonathan, the senior pastor, in his office. He wondered aloud to me, 'What does Ken do all day? All I see him do is sit in Starbucks talking all day with people from the church and the community. What are his plans and programme to move his ministry forward?'" The next day I sat down with Ken at (where else?) Starbucks. Without my mentioning my previous day's conversation with Jonathan, Ken began to wonder out loud also. "Jonathan spends so much time on plans and programs for the church that he rarely takes time to sit down and get to know the church staff or the people in the church. The church staff do not seem to know Jonathan or fully trust him."

The two conversations sum up for me the dilemma we are facing in the Church, or other Christian organisations and the corporate world to some degree. We have two significantly conflicting views of who a leader is and what a leader does. Do we focus on people and programs, or do we put our energy towards fulfilling plans or developing relationships? I think a balance between the two would be a better and effective strategy.

In the past, companies like IBM retained leaders for a lifetime because of a deep loyalty and commitment to the company and its employees. Organisations fostered a culture of loyalty and corporate paternalism. However, as these companies have needed to change because of changing economic and cultural conditions, the loyalty tie has significantly weakened.

THE CHANGING WORLD AROUND US

The World is changing around us so fast that we can hardly keep up. In his book, "The Lexus and the Olive tree", Thomas Friedman states that the post-modern world is just about twenty years old. From his perspective, this new emerging culture had its birth on November 1989, with the tearing down of the Berlin Wall, marking the end of the Cold War. The wall was the symbol of the Cold war, while the Web is the symbol of the emerging culture. The Berlin Wall represented the armed-fortress mentality of the Cold War. The Web represents the boundary-free world of the emerging culture.

In the modern world, symbolised by the Cold War, life was compartmentalised, regimented and strictly organised. Leadership in the corporate world and the Church was highly regimented. For several centuries, leadership was defined by industrial society; we were in the business of producing and making things. Leaders defined themselves as managers. Authority in the modern world was based on rules, roles and organisational structures.

Carl Raschke calls the modern Church "A managed faith body". Leadership was based upon reason and the leader followed the plan. The result is that many existing leaders represent the hierarchical and controlling view of leadership. The emerging culture is much more open, with few restrictions and unlimited opportunities. Bill Gates says, "The only factory asset we have is the human imagination." If the modern leader is represented by a culture of networking, permission giving and empowerment, there are many resources available to give us a more thorough understanding of this change from modern to emerging culture.

77

FROM DIRECTING TO EMPOWERING

Earlier on, we were introduced to Jonathan and Ken; Jonathan's default mode of leadership was to direct, whilst Ken's mode was to empower. Jonathan emphasised clarity of vision, Ken emphasised the building of a community of leaders. Jonathan wanted to lead by giving instructions and directions to the Church. Ken chose to lead through developing community within the Church. Jonathan's leadership resulted in more clarity and control of vision; Ken's leadership resulted in more ownership of the vision. These two opposing views of leadership, which can be complementary, are at the heart of the conflict facing existing and emerging leaders as they attempt to work together on a staff team.

LEADERSHIP MODELS

The Top-Down Controlling Leadership Model: In modern culture, especially the corporate culture of the 20th century, there exists a top-down model of work. The business leaders appropriate a command-and-control method of management and leadership. It results in tremendous growth for the business. Basic management function consists of planning, organising and controlling. The senior leaders of the company, including the board of directors, direct those under them to accomplish the desired growth. The definition of management was "Getting things done through and with other people". The formula for success became "People + Result + Organisation = Satisfaction."

In the last quarter of the 20th century, many growth-oriented churches adopted this business model to grow congregations. As churches (and other ministry organisations that wanted to grow) began to look around for successful models in the 20th century, they turned to the business world, where they saw a growth model that worked. They also turned to the business model because many of the elders and key lay leaders of the Church came from the modern business culture. Thus, the business model was incorporated by most of the fastest-growing churches without asking questions about the appropriateness of their decisions.

The logic of many church leaders was that if it worked for the business world, it should work for the Church. Many of the lay leaders and major donors in the Church came out of the business world. Many of the foundations and donors that supported and still support ministry organisations are embedded in the business world. They are convinced that what has worked in the business world for the last fifty years should continue to work in the Church today. There is a lot of pressure from these key donors and foundations being placed on pastors and ministry leaders to increase church growth numerically.

The bottom line in the business or ministry world is growth. In the business world, growth is measured by financial profit. In the Church world, success is measured by the strength of numerical membership, though it should be noted that numerical growth that does not develop into discipleship, may not be sustainable. In the last quarter of the 20th century, we saw many churches experience significant numerical growth. It is not surprising that more growth in the business world or Church would usually result in more direction or control by its leaders. As Margaret Wheatley suggests about leaders in growing companies, "If we don't take control, there is only chaos. As growth occurs a manager is content on running the organisation as smoothly and as efficiently as it can function. A manager wants to approach the inevitable chaos with tried and true methods that have worked in the past."

Empowering Others: Instead of controlling or directing, empowering is better. The leader's role is not to direct and control but to empower and give away ministry to others, as Apostle Paul admonished in 1Cor 12:27–31.

Most parents would remember their experiences when their children were trying to transit from crawling to walking. On the part of the baby there was the risk of falling down and fell down they did on a number of occasions, but that didn't deter them from trying again. Eventually, they mastered the art of walking and would not want to exchange that for going back to crawling. Slowly, their fear of failure gave way to learning from their failure.

Instead of controlling and directing, we should endeavour to empower. There is a clear correlation between participation and productivity. Jesus certainly looked beyond the chaos of His days to empower the disciples for the future.

BECOMING AN EMPOWERING LEADER

Servant Leadership: Servant Leadership is the opposite of the corporate CEO model, where everyone obeys the big boss. Servant leaders are givers and not takers. They don't hold too tightly to their position of power or title, led by learning from those they lead, and are available to the people they lead.

Larry Spears identifies seven characteristics of the Servant leader – Listening, Empathy, Healing, Conceptualisation, Awareness, Persuasion, and Foresight.

Shared Leadership: In addition to being a servant leader, we should be prepared for shared leadership. Empowerment involves the sharing of power as some authority and decision making is transferred. Delegation, which comes with shared leadership, shows that you are willing and ready to trust others, and if you've trained them well enough, there would be nothing to fear.

Partner Leadership: This involves listening to others. Are we exchanging our strengths and capabilities? No one person can be strong in all areas, so are we exchanging our weaknesses for someone else's strength?

Power Blessing Leadership: Handing the baton to the next set of leaders. This would have to be a deeply thought out process that goes to training and apprenticeship.

Guiding Leadership: A leadership that guides instead of the Control-Command structure. It connects, collaborates, coalesces, converges and communes.

Gifted Leadership: Leadership that equips others to see the potential within themselves and helps to nurture that gift to a state of stability. In modern paradigm, leaders had all the answers, vision and everything else; they did it all. However, in the new paradigm, they equip others for and in ministry.

Trust-Based Leadership: To trust as a leader is to be able to let go, and this again is a fall back from the type of training that people have been infused with. With effective training we are sure the leaders we are producing are ready and capable to take the reins; hence the trust reposed in them.

When structures take precedence over mission, and highly centralised leadership stops people contributing, those who are gifted tend to leave. The most frequent reason emerging leaders give for leaving the Church is controlling leadership.

The mission statement at the office of the city manager, J. Russell Allen, for Raleigh, North Carolina, US, states, "To build an organisation in which control gives way to empowerment, direction gives way to participation and routine gives way to creativity". Any organisation is only as strong as its leader. "A wise leader", says Nancy Ortberg, "Strengthens people by giving power away".

FROM MAP TO COMPASS

In the past, experience was a valued asset for a leader. However, the past no longer is a good guide for the future. Experience is no longer an asset. This thought goes against all that we have been taught about leadership. In the past, leadership experience always trumped inexperience. Today, it could be a handicap. Leonard Sweet says, "Too many church leaders are relying on strategies, methods, information, and systems that are outdated as to be barriers to leadership. The tried and true was true when it was tried, it may be false today". This is not to dismiss that some principles are fundamental and are relevant for all time.

THE EMERGING CHURCH (I-Church)

Here we begin to relate to what the Church looks like today, how Information Technology is transforming the way the Church operates, and the influence of business-related management principles—its upside and downside.

Businesses are Progressing: Brian Humek, in his '21st Century Business and Church Practices', said, "Business practices are changing; so are the ways of the Church." To this end, CEOs now call themselves brand evangelists, they tell the good news of their brand. The importance companies now place on their customers and their desire to add value to the lives of each one is critical. Sometimes this is shown by customising a customer's experience, whether with a website visit or a product.

Are Churches Regressing? In stark contrast, churches are growing larger and expanding to the point that mega churches dot the religious landscape. They look and act as if they were created by a cookie cutter.

Churches now use social media, but typically, only to communicate, not to interact with the social community around them. Then, there is the old 20th century business practice churches sometimes embrace; the practice of only paying attention to those who can do something for you or who have done something for you.

It could be argued that churches are regressing while businesses are progressing in the use of Information technology, but there could be exceptions in both cases. There are businesses who ignore the needs or wants of customers, some which never interact with customers on social media (businesses that could fail). There are also some churches who meet the needs of their members (customers) and those in their community who need help. Some churches even interact on Twitter and Facebook and are very much 21st century as they add value to people's lives. Whether I'm a church visitor (or member) or a potential customer to your business, as Pat Benetar used to sing, "Treat Me Right." "Dear Churches and businesses, pay attention to me. Care about my opinion. Add value to my life. But do it all the time, continuously. Not just when you want something special from me. Because when you do that, it sort of makes me feel a bit dirty. But the Church is to be different from that."

The beautiful thing about the Church is that it is made up of the redeemed of God who have been forgiven…, called out from living as the world does…, been raised to walk in newness of life…, shining as lights in an earth of darkness, and doing the will of God rather than conforming to the world.

There is no need for CEOs or Presidents or Vice Presidents in the Church—KING Jesus is the one and only Church Executive Officer (Col 1:16–18). There is no need to confine our fellowship and our praises to Him to 60 minutes of Business Time. Every second of our existence is His! There is no point in wanting more and more money. Every cent/pence we have comes from Him and belongs to Him. Our ambition should not be limited to just climbing the corporate ladder in our desire to succeed. In Christ, each disciple is wealthy beyond imagination (2 Corinthians 8:9).

If we take a close, honest look at most of the latter-day Charismatic/Pentecostal Churches, how many of these business philosophies would we find at play? Is the Church driven by the things above or by the things below? There is the need for balance between making the Church become too people-focused—where all we are doing is management systems—and dynamism of the human knowledge—where the Holy Ghost has no space or place to operate. At the same time, we ought to be careful, and not present the Church as this sanctimonious, earthly-irrelevant, heaven-bound body, whose sole purpose is to go to heaven.

In any case, it is wise to constantly ask ourselves, which is having the greater impact—the Church on the world or the world on the Church? I hope the Church is influencing the world and not the other way round. I pray that as the Church, I am influencing the world rather than the world influencing me.

Paul certainly became "All things to all men so he could, by all means, save some" (1 Corinthians 9:22). Yet, that did not stop him from identifying the earthly philosophies that invaded the thinking of the Church so that she could repent and grow (1 Corinthians 1:10−13, 5:1−6, 6:1−8; Galatians 1:10; Philippians 2:3−7; 1 Thessalonians 4:1−7). But since the Church has always been made up of people who inevitably fall short, as we are not perfect in every way as our Father is, we must constantly test ourselves and consistently take inventory of the principles we are clinging to; checking that the principles we are abiding by and living by are the commands of Christ not the commandments and traditions of men.

A PASTOR VS THE BUSINESSPERSON

What, if any, are the comparisons/differences between a pastor and a businessperson? The line between ministry and the business world has blurred. It is increasingly difficult to tell the difference between secular and sacred leadership, and there are some influential voices arguing that any differentiation is artificial. As a result, many pastors have eagerly sought the wisdom of business leaders to help them manage their churches. But what if the tables were reversed? Could a pastor successfully lead in a business environment?

In an online publication, Andy Rowell examined this position, referring to the legendary former CEO of General Electric (GE), Jack Welch, who wrote an article on "Leaving the Non-profit Nest" (Business Week). In the said article, Welch recounts the story of a woman who has tried to move from a non-profit organisation (Think "Church") into the business world, she got nowhere. The reason he alludes to this is because the business world has not had much success with people from the non-profit world. He believes the fundamental problem is that non-profit people cannot adjust to a competitive environment. They make decisions too slowly and do not care enough about results. Still, Jack says, the non-profit person has some skills that are unique— primarily, the ability to manage people without having money as a motivational tool.

Some of the issues that can be raised are:

1. Do pastors with a competitive background—perhaps having significant sports or business experience— lead with a greater focus on numbers in the church? And is this an asset or something to be cautious about? Does this explain the difference between pastors who shepherd and pastors who lead? Yes, pastors are to be aware of their competitive bent. If they are to drive to see their congregation "win," that is an appropriate desire. But "winning" should be defined

appropriately. The Church should produce better and more disciples of Christ who live sacrificially. Winning isn't about the ABC's (Attendance, Buildings, and Cash).

2. Some pastors fantasise that if their church career doesn't work out they can simply grab a job in the business world. But is that true? Is Jack Welch right when he says most leaders in the non-profit sector could not hack it in the business world and should choose something softer? The truth is God has directed people to his work for all kinds of reasons. Still, pastors can accept the criticism that churches can become unfocused and perpetuate mediocrity if not careful.

3. Does Welch's impression of non-profits manifest itself in our congregations when members (perhaps with a business background) get frustrated by the committees and lowest common denominator decision-making? It is hard to disagree with Welch's criticism, but that doesn't mean we should run the Church like a business. It does mean, however, that these Christians with savvy business sense may help us make decisions more quickly. Perhaps if we listened to them more we would have more time for prayer, pastoral care, Scripture and ministry toward the poor.

4. Welch points out the challenge of leading people without money as an incentive. What does that leave the pastor in his leadership arsenal? How do we motivate, and does this make a pastor's relational

skills the critical factor? The reality is that most pastors must lead without much positional authority— this varies, of course. Some traditions still give the pastoral office a significant amount of authority. If a pastor presses for change too quickly, they may be run out within a year. Therefore, pastors must be able to lead collaboratively (helping others feel ownership for decisions), inspirationally (keeping people's spirits up about the mission) and subversively (persuading people to do what is right even when the people's first response is flowing from a desire to be comfortable). Pastors who are able to lead effectively are some of the most impressive leaders on the planet.

On the surface, I would say "AMEN" to the thought of pastors being more competitive. However, the rules of engagement and what the actual results look like many times cannot be compared to business. A typical business is not obligated to care for people when times are lean. A pastor cannot just slash a division in one five-minute meeting. He cannot motivate, as stated, with money. People have to be led by vision and altruism. So, we do need to be about results, however, simply looking at a budget or attendance are not the only indicators. Changed lives need to be seen and this takes more than giving bonuses or threatening layoffs.

Whereas leadership, when it is good, can fit into any setting, business management does not necessarily apply to the way a church is managed; as much as some would like to say it does. It could be argued that the role of the pastor is not to control what people do in the sense of a bottom line, as we see in business. It could also be said that the role of a pastor is to empower people to serve in the world in such a way that others are drawn to Christ.

As Christians, we are dependent on the work of the Holy Spirit, and we are also to be equipped for the works that God has prepared in advance for us to do. Sometimes that is hard to measure. Is it about the number of baptisms this year? Is it about confessions of faith? Or is it about how many of our newly converted members have shared their faith with a friend or co-worker and/or led a friend or co-worker to a commitment of faith. Or is it just about faithfulness, no matter how effective we are? Is being ineffectively faithful good enough? In asking these questions we are trying to imagine that they are being asked of us as we look the LORD in the eyes. Changed lives that end up impacting other lives is emerging as a good measure of a healthy church; the kind of church we should strive to see.

This question must also be asked: Are Pastors collaborative enough? The issue here is effectiveness, not competition. We must confront the lie that people do their best when working against, rather than with each other. And while competition can improve efficiency, this alone doesn't guarantee effectiveness. Working in the military has similar challenges (motivating people beyond money); and indecision and lack of commitment can have devastating consequences. Many military leaders would also not cut it in the business world (Not necessarily a bad thing, neither do bean-counters belong on the battlefield!).

Church leaders need to draw from the full diversity of New Testament metaphors—commercial and domestic, household, priesthood, family, even army—to cultivate faithfulness. It cannot but be noticed that some of the leaders with the most vibrant churches think and talk like business people.

What these pastors have that many pastors lack is the disciplined thinking it takes to focus their church's efforts and to make the difficult decisions. Too many pastors are crippled by the need to make everyone happy. The end result of this handicap is a lack of focus and a leadership by consensus approach that is not leadership at all.

That said, a corporation's singular goal is to maximise shareholder value (make money). The decisions required to maximise financial outputs at times necessarily conflict with the Church's expressed goal of creating a different kind of output (disciples, a better world, etc.). While some of the same principles apply, it is dangerous to assume that an adoption of the corporate mind set will lead us to spiritual prosperity. We must think critically about this, taking the good and leaving behind those elements that would transform an organism into a machine.

Jack Welch postulating says, "Pastors might make lousy businesspeople"—well, that is open to debate. But by turning the table round, imagine a church led by "Pastor Jack Welch"—interesting thought. The concept of leadership in the Church would continue to be an interesting and evolving one. Part of the concepts in organisational management are relevant in the Church today—emotional intelligence, collaborative skills, communicating skills, drawing a distinction between competition and collaboration.

We are called the light of the world and as light we illuminate, so we are supposed to add value to the world system. Yes, God has given us human beings the capacity to reason and think, that is where some of the principles we admire in the secular world arises. However, we have a higher and greater calling and since the one who called us created all we admire and can see in the world today, as Christian leaders we can and ought to do better. The role of competition in the life and ministry of a pastor is an important topic. I think pastors ought to be competitive, but that competitiveness should be aimed squarely at sin, death and the devil, not other churches or leaders.

CONCLUSION

Yes, there are management principles that are applicable and important in the administration of the Church. After all, God has given us wisdom to benefit ourselves and improve the Church and our relationship with him. However, the role of the Holy Spirit should be acknowledged and appreciated. John 16:12–13 says that "When the spirit of truth is come, He would lead us into ALL truth." Another passage (John 14:6), says, "I am the way, the truth and the life", so in as much as there is a human or an intellectual role we play, we cannot ignore the supernatural, where God himself enthrones His Church. He says, "I will build My Church and the gates of hell shall not prevail against it", Matt 16:16−18. The challenge is being able to know where man finishes and God starts, and drawing the defining line between human effort and God's input.

Hence as Christians who are businessmen/women, our values reflect the faith we profess. Our faith is a way of life, and as such it should affect and influence the decisions we make. We should behave as custodians who would have to give an account of his/her stewardship.

Our Christian walk (which is one throughout our lives) should inform our decisions as stewards who would be giving account of their stewardship. After all, if it is our business, wealth, possessions—whatever, there is nothing we brought into the world and we shall take nothing away. Yes, we ought to strive to be all we have been called to be. But, whilst we are doing that we should do it within the perimeter of what God has called us to be.

Yes, there is and there can be a healthy nexus between the Church and the Marketplace; one that is mutually benefitting to both parties and makes it a win-win situation.

REFERENCES

Adams, Bridget and Raithatha, Manoj. (2012) *"Building the Kingdom through Business"*, Evangelical Alliance Website, Kindle version.

Andy Rodwell, Associate Pastor in Vancouver, British Columbia, also Doctor of Theology at the Duke School concentrating on *Leading Christian Communities and the New Testament.*

Brian Thomas Humek (2014). *21st Century Business and Church Practices.*

Cross, F.L, and Livingstone, E.A. (1909) *The Oxford Dictionary of the Christian Church.*

Donovan, P. (2012) *Church outline moral compass for business.*

Henry, Thorne Sell (1854–1928). Studies in early Church history (Online series).

DK (2015) How Business Works – *A Graphic Guide to Business Success*, Penguin Random House.

Investopedia.com, online publication on Investments.

Jeffrey Weber (2012) From Idea to Exit, *The Entrepreneurial Journey.*

Jimmy, Long. (2009), *The Leadership Jump–Building Partnership between Existing and Emerging Christian Leaders,* Downes Grove, ILL: Inter Varsity Press.

Jones, Rufus. M. George Fox (2006) *An Autobiography, Friends* United Press. ISBN 0-913408-24-7.

Lawrence, Bill. *"Titus: Live Like a Man, Lead like Men"*, Bible.org, http://www.leaderformation.org

Levy, Barry (1988) *Quakers and the American Family: British Settlement in the Delaware Valley*, New York. Oxford University Press.

Lunn-Rockliffe Sophie (Dr), *Christianity and the Roman Empire* (BBC Archives).

Milligan, Edward H. (2007) *The Biographical Dictionary of British Quakers in Commerce and Industry*, 1775-1920.

Online Publication, *"Ask Church Leaders"*, Hoolenbach

Peter, B. Clarke. (1993) *World's Religions, Understanding the Living Faith*, Reader's Digest Series).

Rowan, Williams. (2012) *Faith in the Public Square. Former Archbishop of the Church of England, Bloomsbury* (2012).

Sara Williams, Financial Times Guide (Business Start-up, 2017–2018)

DK (2014) *The Business Book Big Ideas, Simply Explained*, (Eds); Richard Gilbert, Diana Loxley, Sara Tomley, Marek Walisiewicz.

WhatIs.com, post by Magaret Rouse.

Windsor, DB (1980), *The Quaker Enterprise: Friends in Business*, Federick Muller Ltd, London, ISBN 0-584-102257-7.